TO THE WREN

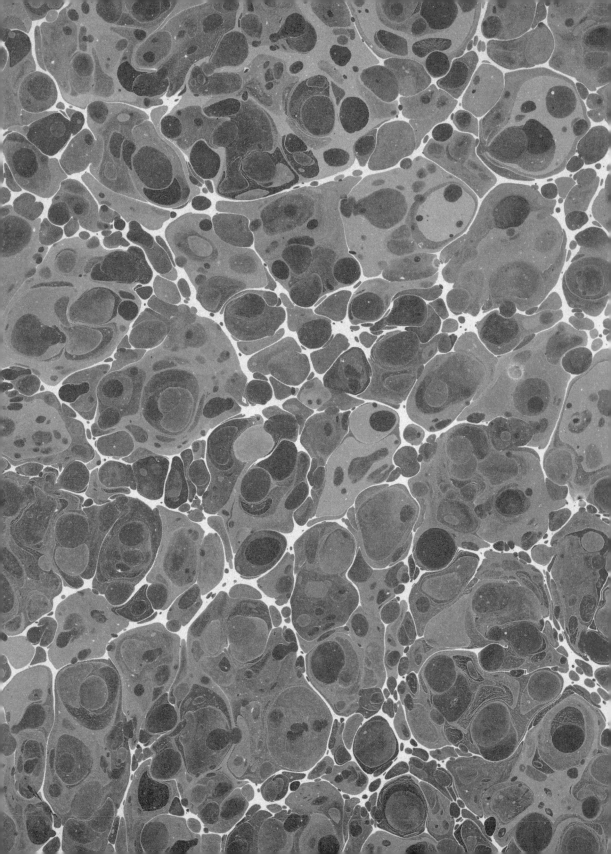

TO THE WREN

COLLECTED & NEW POEMS

1991-2019

JANE MEAD

Alice James Books
Farmington, Maine
www.alicejamesbooks.org

10 9 8 7 6 5 4 3 2 1

Alice James Books are published by Alice James Poetry Cooperative, Inc., an affiliate of the University of Maine at Farmington.

Alice James Books
114 Prescott Street
Farmington, ME 04938
www.alicejamesbooks.org

Library of Congress Cataloging-in-Publication Data

Names: Mead, Jane, 1958- author.
Title: To the wren : collected & new poems 1991-2019 / Jane Mead.
Other titles: Poems
Description: Farmington, ME : Alice James Books, [2019] | Includes indexes.
Identifiers: LCCN 2018044242 (print) | LCCN 2018052119 (ebook) | ISBN
    9781948579575 (eBook) | ISBN 9781948579018 (pbk. : alk. paper)
Classification: LCC PS3563 (ebook) | LCC PS3563 .E165 2019 (print) | DDC
    811/.54--dc23
LC record available at https://lccn.loc.gov/2018044242

Alice James Books gratefully acknowledges support from individual donors, private foundations, the University of Maine at Farmington, the National Endowment for the Arts, and the Amazon Literary Partnership.

Cover art: University of Washington Libraries, Special Collections, UW37568

for my teachers
and for my students

For the sake of accurately preserving their evolution,
I have chosen not to alter these poems in any way
from how they appeared when first published in book form.
—Jane Mead

TABLE OF CONTENTS

A TRUCK MARKED FLAMMABLE (1991)

THE LORD AND THE GENERAL DIN OF THE WORLD (1996)

THREE

HOUSE OF POURED-OUT WATERS (2001)

1.

THE USABLE FIELD (2008)

I

II

MONEY MONEY MONEY | WATER WATER WATER (2014)

THAT THE CHURCH OF ENGLAND
SHOULD BE FREE

FALLEN LEAF LAKE

DOROTHY PRETENDING TO BE WATER
DOROTHY PRETENDING TO BE SKY

WORLD OF MADE AND UNMADE (2016)

NEW POEMS (2019)

A TRUCK MARKED FLAMMABLE

—for Edith Morgan Whitaker

Special thanks to Aspen Rose Ahmad.—

A TRUCK MARKED FLAMMABLE

(From inside the dumpster,
outside the bughouse)

HEADNOTES

1 Euclid assumed the truth of five postulates, upon which he built his system of geometry. The fifth of these postulates was troublesome, both to Euclid and to subsequent mathematicians and, since he could not prove it, he avoided using it as much as possible. By 1763 twenty-eight faulty proofs of the fifth postulate had been published. In 1823, Non-Euclidean geometry was discovered by twenty-one-year-old János Bolyai, and, simultaneously, by Nokolay Lobachevskiy. It was based, not on a proof of the fifth postulate, but on a denial of it, and a following out of the consequences of that denial. In the following letter, Farkas Bolyai, father to János, describes the frustrations of his own lifelong attempts at trying, unsuccessfully, to prove Euclid's fifth postulate. (See Douglas R. Hofstadter, *Gödel, Escher, Bach* (New York: Vintage Books, 1979), pp. 88-99.)

2 Joseph Campbell, *The Hero with a Thousand Faces* (Princeton: Princeton University Press, 1986), p. 42.

3 In their *Principia Mathematica*, Bertrand Russell and Alfred North Whitehead set out to rid logic, set theory, and number theory from paradoxes. In order to do this they had to eliminate self-reference between terms within any given system. They created closed systems which relied on extremely formal and artificial definitions in order to rid these systems of paradoxes. For example, they rid set theory of its paradoxes by disallowing the formation of certain kinds of sets. In 1931 Gödel published a paper in which he showed that no axiomatic system could be proven consistent without the imposition of such artificial rules. (See Hofstadter, pp. 18-24.)

You must not attempt this approach to parallels. I know this way to its very end. I have traversed this bottomless night, which extinguished all light and joy of my life. I entreat you, leave the science of parallels alone . . . I thought I would sacrifice myself for the sake of the truth. I was ready to become a martyr who would remove the flaw from geometry and return it purified to mankind. I accomplished monstrous, enormous labors; my creations are far better than those of others and yet I have not achieved complete satisfaction. For here it is true that *si paullum a summo discessit, vergit adimum.**

I turned back unconsoled, pitying myself and all mankind . . . I have traveled past all reefs of this infernal Dead Sea and have always come back with broken mast and torn sail. The ruin of my disposition and my fall date back to this time. I thoughtlessly risked my life and happiness—*aut Caesar aut nihil.***[1]

*If he comes down a bit from the heights, he swerves towards the bottom.

**Either Caesar or Nothing.

I

The nurses make my name

into a song
because they like to hear
their own voices singing.

MAArio ... MAAArio,
MAAArio GallUUUCHio.
And when I hear them I hug my knees
more tightly to my chest—
my butt pulls me deeper
into the soggy layers
where it's quiet. Everything shifts
slightly; the flies all jump
into the air where they will wait
for me to resettle.
Then I close my eyes
and the color is the same
dark gray as these walls.
I squeeze my eyes. I make the colors
of orange peels and banana skins.

They see a forest green
dumpster. When they walk past
their song rises
and falls through the air—
but my absence holds
its place against them:
a pocket of air, resting
in the dead branches
of the tree across the lot,
my absence *never* shifts, no matter
what the wind says.

Usually I'm in the rec room
when that clumsy truck
bitches its way up the drive.
I go to the window and watch it
lift my box and dump
everything into itself—
the place I hollowed out,
the walls and floor I made
just so. Everything but a few
useless globs that stick
or snail down the steel walls.
Then it's two days before
I have enough to work with,
three before it's right
in here again.

One day in April, while the snow
was being changed into mud
and the grass lured back into life,
I spent my morning hours sorting
plastic forks and knives,
gallon milk jugs, and juice tins
with bright pictures of ripe oranges
peeling from their sides
from the paper plates and cups
that I crushed into a leaf-like nest.
I curled up, let the warm smell
cover me and slept.
The truck's beeping and whining
woke me—just in time. I climbed out

the back door, without peeking first—
but nobody saw me.

Some days, I am a lucky man.

II
Today I told the doctor

I wanted to be
a girl eating salad, just
a girl eating salad—
idly looking out a window,
idly watching the traffic,
watching the traffic
without a thought—
eating salad.

If he understood me
he did not say.
He did say,
however (as they say)
"you are, however, not."

III
Till I was four

my parents kept me in the rabbit hutch
at the far end of the lawn on Sunday
afternoons for safekeeping.
I read this in a report on me.

But what I remember is the way
I graphed my world as it moved
beyond the wire's sturdy grid
without knowing, without needing
to know, the name for what I did.
I remember my mother's head
at the kitchen window, swaying
in a gentle arc as she ironed,
my father pacing out the X-axis
with his big boots, running his head
along the fifth grid, and back
and out of sight where the lawnmower
still sputtered. And I remember
how those soft-bodied rabbits
whom I loved, loved me.
And, one day in particular,
how we watched the bright leaves falling,
as they must have fallen often.

In time I might have learned something
more about what passes between
the wind and a leaf
when the leaf is falling.
With a stopwatch and a ruler
on the grid, I could have learned,
by the time I was seven

to figure the speed of one leaf
falling on one calm Sunday
and known then something
of the order in an instant.

But when I was four, a man
with a heavy holster and stiff pants
got out of a blue and white car
and waved his papers at my father's face.
And then, my father pulled me out
of that straw bed and bought
a padlock to keep me out and I
had to touch my rabbits
from the other side
of the wire's sturdy grid.
Within a week they lost interest
in me, and there was nothing I could do
to coax their little squares of fur,
their mobile noses, to the front of the hutch.
I began to wander
the complicated lawn.

So, I grew up somewhere
between points east and west
in the generation of the professional
backrub, in a town marked
"gas only," in a two story white house
near highway 80, never dreaming
that the numbers would not step in
and show the way in which all things
explain themselves in relation

to each other, thinking only
that if I worked and worked
and worked them they'd help me
understand the traffic on the highway,
the slant of the roof, the hardened
white drip on the paint can.

By the time I was ten I'd begun
ordering my days around the joy
of every proof I could coax out
of the postulates, but when I was
fourteen the postulates collapsed
and fell like questions at my feet
and I began the lonely work of proving
the given, as if the world depended
on me for its existence. But sometimes,
buoyed up towards my dreamful sleep,
I sensed the shy presence
of some lamenting God—
just on the verge of speaking.

IV

But even Euclid couldn't prove
his faulty fifth; it was
the prayer he built his dreams on
and on his dreams they built
the Golden Gate, which hovers
over the silver bay—God's
answer to the doubtful.
Mario, I told myself, you
must learn to see
God's voice; you must learn
to pray, and he will answer.

V
So, I prayed

at the university. I used formulas
that worked like machines
greased to a point past friction,
making jumbles of numbers
fall evenly into place.
Sometimes I worked at my desk
through the night with nothing
to disturb me but the sound
of the night watchman
who'd jingle slowly up the hall,
like a dog with too many tags
to surprise a cat, turn his key
at a quarter past each hour
and jingle slowly away
with his steady steps and his gun—
reminding me that I should have been
home hours ago, pulling chicken
from the cracks between my teeth.

Stepping out in the morning
after those nights
it was always as if it had just
rained, as if it were spring
and a subway token an unusually
bright and dispensable thing.
I welled up right smack
to behind my eyes and
had to lower my lashes
on the platform. The world was
that close and I was
that close to it—I wanted not

to come out through my eyes
in such a dim unruly place.
Do you know what it means
when all the numbers take their places
and insist upon their innocence
amid the chaotic babble about paradoxes?
When the pourers of concrete
defy the smashers of theory
(when a building scrapes the sky,
when a bridge casts its shadow
on water, when stars and satellites
mix in the heavens, one and the same
to the human eye) it is the numbers,
telling of an invisible shape—an order
so huge and flawless it cannot be seen
clearly in the mind, which it visits
sometimes, in flashes. It is the shadow,
in concrete, of a perfection
no mind can hold.

And if you laugh at me I will count
slowly from one to ten
on the fingers God gave me,
ploddingly, on the fingers
which used to flower geometrically
towards Eden, and remind you—
those formulas work.
Witness the Golden Gate:
good enough for jumping from,

good enough for driving on—
only a fool would rather swim,
choose to scoff a fact
because his mind can't prove it.
The building in the sky. The bridge
on the water. The light
in the heavens. I was so happy
loving my formulas—
but only in flashes.

***

The dome of heaven rests on the quarters of the earth, sometimes supported by four caryatidal kings, dwarfs, giants, elephants or turtles. Hence, the traditional importance of the mathematical problem of the quadrature of the circle: it contains the secret of the transformation of heavenly into earthly forms.[2]

***

VI

And in those flashes
I saw all
that I could not see
with my flawed reason
and I saw
that my reason was flawed,
and shouted

> *damn Russell, damn Whitehead, logic*
> *is of a human mind, while the numbers,*
> *the numbers are divine*
> *I will sing my two shoes, my feet,*
> *my socks that match, my two legs—*
> *one for each leg of my pants—*
> *I will sing the shape of my calculator*
> *and the lopsided circle of the moon.*
> *My absence will hold its place against you.*[3]

VII

Most of you have something

in common with the nurses:
it gives you your knack
for seeing things and leaving
them at that. It makes
everything possible:
the long subway tunnels buried
in the earth, the life of rising
each morning and taking yourself
to work. It stands between
the platform and the platform's
stunning wonder and makes
all things which cross your vision
bearable. In it you see
a perfect blueprint of the world
which shields you from the world's
perfection. It has no name I know of,
for it's all you can see
if you don't know it's there,
but, like a huge mirror,
it reflects all things straight
back to you clearly,
save your own image
which it frees to wander.
Yes. A mirror. That's it.
And like a thought or a mind
it could break when you
least expect it.

VIII

I thought the numbers
would explain the true
workings of God's shadow
on the earth—but I
cannot explain them
and still I sensed Him
somewhere, moving beyond
the clear limits
of my perception.

IX

After I left the university

in New York, I hired out
to drive a truck marked
"flammable" all the way
to San Francisco.

In a truckstop.
In Pittsburgh.
In my little room.
I don't know how it happened,
but I sat on the bed and watched
the slow motion cracking
of that safe blueprint—
my mirror vision of a room:
the web of light creeping
over the table, spreading
past the bathroom door,
'till the whole room starred
and shattered into brightness.
I watched, shocked, as if
I'd sped up a bank into
a wide unyielding tree, as if
it had nothing to do with me—
that ending.

X

I have cursed God
for showing me all
that I cannot see,
for flaunting Himself
through the great machine
of the world, while I
with my flawed understanding
have the power he denied
all other creatures
to recognize my flaw.
And he has,
in turn, cursed me
with a vision
that blinds my eyes.
And now I will fly.

XI

I left the truckstop and drove

that tanker through the narrow streets
of Pittsburgh where a skinny kid
with a scab on his nose
ran after a bus and, falling,
showed no signs on his face
(elsewhere and slightly sad)
that he had fallen, but just
rose up running, token in hand,
through the fumes.
Then a pockmarked kid,
no more than seventeen,
wobbled by on a red bike
balancing an infant
on the rusted handlebars—
one hand on the baby's waist,
laughing, and for a moment
life seemed beautiful
and bright and cheap.

I drove through the narrow streets
of Pittsburgh to a spanky-clean
shopping plaza where I bought
glue and balsa wood,
sand paper and monocoat,
books on gliders, books on wind
and every kind of hopeful thing—
and back, again, I drove
to the truckstop
where I stayed two weeks
in my little room with the window
and the exhausted desk

in the silence that follows
an explosion, while the air resettles
and you begin to feel
for your arms and legs.

I made a glider:
four feet long,
tail and rudder, blue
for the sky. Wings, yellow
for the sun—but translucent
to show their birdlike bones,
a skeleton of spars and ribs,
just so. The fuselage, red breasted
for the birds in the nest
outside Denny's. I made the joints
flush, sanded the curves smooth.
And finally I hung it from the ceiling
and with small fishing weights
I made the balance perfect.

At first launching
my glider soared upwards,
caught in the air
for an instant while my breath
caught in my chest, still
as numbers which have fallen,
forever, into place. As I
let go my breath
the glider stalled,
then dove straight
into the ground.

XII

It soared.
It caught
and hung, hung
and dove
and dove and then
suddenly I realized
all that it meant

to be human.

XIII

And it seemed that neither wind

nor sleep nor thought
could free me
or ease the moments
upon me. I drove my tanker
to a cliff at the edge
of the sea, and set
my postulates in bottles
rolling on the gray waves
out of sight.

Nothing left but me
in the sea's presence, the sea
where the postulates,
all five, were churning.

Then half way to my truck
the pound pound
pounding of the waves
came upon me. I turned;
I left my clothes
on clover. The wind
ripped in off the sea
past cliff and field,
sky of mist filled
the space between
and the waves rolled in gray
off the water like waves
rolling in gray off water.
I stood there
naked, breathing.

XIV

Now I am a man

in a dumpster. Mario,
I tell myself, relax.
In what way
could it possibly matter?
In what way possible,
for in the mind there are many
streets to be mapped.
I tell my thoughts—fly fly,
the beauty of the air
is just today, and everything
my vision crosses is a perfect reflection
of the bright place it came from.
But when they ask me to explain
my naked song and dance
my thoughts just stick.

The voices of the nurses sing by me.
Mario, MAArio,
they call me.
MAAArio, MAAAArio,
flinging their sound
at my ears.
Let them sing.
I let them sing.
My one secret:
where I do my thinking.

If only Einstein had made clear
the lack of friction
in the birds competing in the nest:

the way the world without man
is a cruel but hateless machine
well greased for the shifting of pain.
Then I might be able to begin
to explain something
of the order which surrounds me.

THE LORD AND THE
GENERAL DIN OF THE WORLD

FOREWORD

In an early review of William Carlos Williams' great book, Randall Jarrell wrote, "The subject of *Paterson* is: How can you tell the truth about things?—that is, how can you find a language so close to the world that the world can be represented and understood in it?" That search for language is the same one Jane Mead conducts in her extraordinary first book *The Lord and the General Din of the World*, but the truths Mead tells have less to do with the sights, smells, and sounds of a place and far more to do with the taste of loss, grief, and madness in a community that has spun out of control. In many of her poems that community is a community of two rather than a city, and we, the readers, eavesdrop on a passionate internalized debate that is about no more and no less than the question of whether or not we should live and, should we choose to, how we might go about it.

There are no easy answers in the world in which Mead has grown into her difficult adulthood, but in her poems the natural world is bodied forth in its splendor and beauty and we live just on the brink of joining it. It is a frontier she rarely crosses:

> I'm the one who's always fasting
> as if God would then come in,
> the one with twigs snarled in her hair
> watching a penful of pigs.
> They lie in the mud shitting themselves
> and squinting at me. I love them
> because nothing can do *pig* as well as pig
> and I am lost and do not know who I am, or if
> life has anything to do with prayer.
> ("Between Self and Century")

But even on her side of the frontier between the sacred natural world and the clouded human one certain truths must be stated, and she states them with clarity and assurance in one of the most startling poems in the collection, "Concerning That Prayer I Cannot Make":

> Listen—
> all you bare trees
> burrs

brambles
pile of twigs
red and green lights flashing
muddy bottle shards
shoe half buried—listen

listen, I am holy.

These poems are driven forward by the knowledge that we could hear the meaning of the world in all things, including ourselves, if only we were given the power to listen. "Lord," she asks in the title poem, "is the general din of the world your own?" This "steady grating," as she calls it, is made up of the united voices of all that otherwise might be inconsequential—a plastic bottle, a concrete gutter, tiny waves in a swimming pool—as well as the agonized cries of a human voice.

Even in their most placid moments these poems teeter on the edge of violence as the poet's mind circles around a center of dread. At a poetry lounge (whatever that is) in Berkeley, Mead observes a man reading English pastoral poetry to himself and wonders if the smooth iambs soothe him. Though Mead is immersed in poetry, it is her allergies she is aware of. She wonders if the birds have appeared yet in those pastoral poems, but because her mind is always centered on catastrophe the mere suggestion of larks and nightingales reminds her of Flanders and Picardy, the sites of the horrendous battles of WW I. "The Man in the Poetry Lounge" is a poem that questions the value of poetry itself; it contains no final answer.

Contemplating the late poetry of Thomas Hardy, the English poet Edward Thomas wrote that Hardy's work contained "ninety-nine reasons for not living. Yet it is not a book of despair." I doubt there are ninety-nine reasons in this collection, though it is not a joyous book—very few contemporary poetry collections are—but it too is not a cause for despair. It is because in these poems we suffer a world of madness, addiction, and death that the moments of redemption are so charged and significant. In "After Detox" she writes:

In the morning, sitting in my nightgown by the window,
I watch the light seep around the corners of Glen's Garage.
Yellow, orange, blue. Colors of the rainbow
or the sky rising. Colors on the rusted plates
on the rusted cars. Cars with their toes turned up,
tires sold, fenders missing. Cars from all over, with maps
of stars on the windshields where heads have smashed.

As you can hear, Mead is determined not to let us off easily; even the most serene moments are stained with the human, but these poems possess the uncanny ability to discover beauty where we almost never see it, in the least honored and most despised places.

Finally, it should be stated emphatically: This is poetry. Perhaps it does not contain a surplus of those details we associate with poetry. There are no swains here, though there is a man at the LaGuardia Airport holding an iris. You won't find elms, but there are cottonwoods. The sea makes an appearance. Children enter, a blood-stained needle, vineyards, dying young men, a truckload of chickens on the way to market, a father armed and threatening. Mead's work does not rely on a special or exalted vocabulary. You won't find those "auras" or "angels" that turn up so often in today's fashionable poetry. There is not a single Buddha in the entire collection, but the language is as alive and unpredictable as a cat, though sometimes in its stubbornness and truculence it reminds one more of a badger:

> If I put in the part about my mother
> and step-father fighting, if I describe
> —perfectly—his body in action,
> his shadow on the wall behind him,
> or add the bit about it all boiling down
> to inquisitions in the rational morning—as in
> whose dark anus holds the safe-box key—
> will we have a story with a meaning?
> ("LaGuardia, the Story")

Her language is a constant source of delight and alarm. It seldom crosses the page in order to entertain us. It prefers to leap out of its own darkness with the suddenness of something wild and catch us by the throat. It is what poetry has always been, risky and untamable.

Philip Levine
Fresno, July 1995

CONCERNING THAT PRAYER I CANNOT MAKE

Jesus, I am cruelly lonely
and I do not know what I have done
nor do I suspect that you will answer me.

And, what is more, I have spent
these bare months bargaining
with my soul as if I could make her
promise to love me when now it seems
that what I meant when I said "soul"
was that the river reflects
the railway bridge just as the sky
says it should—it speaks *that* language.

I do not know who you are.

I come here every day
to be beneath this bridge,
to sit beside this river,
so I *must* have seen the way
the clouds just slide
under the rusty arch—
without snagging on the bolts,
how they are borne along on the dark water—
I must have noticed their fluent speed
and also how that tattered blue T-shirt
remains snagged on the crown
of the mostly sunk dead tree
despite the current's constant pulling.
Yes, somewhere in my mind there must
be the image of a sky blue T-shirt, caught,
and the white islands of ice flying by

and the light clouds flying slowly
under the bridge, though today the river's
fully melted. I must have seen.

But I did not see.

I am not equal to my longing.
Somewhere there should be a place
the exact shape of my emptiness—
there should be a place
responsible for taking one back.
The river, of course, has no mercy—
it just lifts the dead fish
toward the sea.

Of course, of course.

What I *meant* when I said "soul"
was that there should be a place.

On the far bank the warehouse lights
blink red, then green, and all the yellow
machines with their rusted scoops and lifts
sit under a thin layer of sunny frost.

And look—
my own palm—
there, slowly rocking.
It is *my* pale palm—
palm where a black pebble
is turning and turning.

Listen—
all you bare trees
burrs
brambles
pile of twigs
red and green lights flashing
muddy bottle shards
shoe half buried—listen

listen, I am holy.

ONE

THE LORD AND THE GENERAL DIN OF THE WORLD

The kids are shrieking at the edge of the pool,
their angelic faces twisting. They like
to shriek—they like to make the Great Dane bellow.
When he cannot stand it any longer, he jumps
the wall and chases them, still screaming, in.

And under all this now a steady grating—
a plastic bottle of blue cheese dressing
scraping up against the concrete gutter,
bobbing off the aqua, sun-flicked waves
the kids have made by jumping.

And there's a man here from Afghanistan
who hasn't cut his greasy hair since he was driven mad.
His name is Simon. He looks just like The Christ.
Walks up and down beside the pool, oblivious
to screams and barking. He gestures as he talks,
whispers and pontificates. No one is listening.

Lord, is the general din of the world your own?
Something that is good in me is crumbling.

Early this morning I walked out into the vineyard
where the sun hits the sunburnt grapeleaves
and the dusty grapes about to be harvested.
I felt something light then—the skittish joy
that is also a falling off from the world
to that place you can get to by fasting.

Simon marches by, then stops—and looks
at a stretch of bright green grass:

"Is that shit?
I thought so.
I have been here before.
They always hide the horses though."

What holds me here destroys me as I go.

FALL

for Aspen and Shaheen

This morning I found
a used needle in the empty box
marked *produce* in the empty
icebox, sponged the blood speck
from its tip. The fog pushed at the windows
with a sickening heave. I picked
another moth from the drain.

To pick a moth from a sink
for the pain its flight might waken
in the mind's tepid stagnation
is a desperate act.
But last night I sat on the concrete floor
watching flies on the toilet seat,
and listened to my father, who was up
in the loft breathing hayseed
and waving his .38 at the place
where the north star should have been—
shouting at my cousin who'd gone down
to Santa Cruz with scabs
the size of nickels on her feet
to trade her baby for someone's Porsche,
and I have forgotten
what it is to be human.
What it is to be human:
I forget the dusted wings, the whiff
of sage on the fog; I forget
that an action could be made
to make meaning.

Did I choose
the humiliation of my own blood,
this hiding in shirtsleeves?

If this moth could shock me
I might remember that half-thought
before I smoked my first cigarette
at the top of the vineyard
fifteen years ago—that split
second when I sensed
I was choosing—or that fleeting
tug the first night I rummaged
in the tack room for a horse needle.

There is a strange world
in the changing of a light bulb,
the waxing of a bookshelf
I think I could grow by,
as into a dusty dream
in which each day layers
against one just past
and molds the one to come,
content as cabbage
drudging towards harvest.

It may be too far
to get to.
This morning my sister's children
knocked on the door—
I said I was sleeping; my eyes
were crusted wild and they said "but

Aunt Jane, we don't have
mud on our feet, please
can't we come in?"

Their terrifying, trusting voices
come back and back.

If I stepped outside
now, I could watch them
pedaling up and down
the foggy rows of vines,
their eyes clear
and open wide. Someday
I would like to write something
beautiful for them,
a song of order, undrunk,
but livable, a song
of frogs tonguing into themselves
the quiet deaths of flies, of nights
needing days, a song
equal to this season.

WHERE THE ZINFANDEL PASS THEIR SEASONS IN MUTE ROWS

The night Ed died, my father
wrenched his own
cracked, yellow molars
from his mouth and went
crashing like a wounded deer
over the ridge and down,
five miles through the brush,
into Soda Canyon where the cops
found him wandering, spent,
around the burnt-out dance hall
and brought him home.

Bandaging his brush cuts,
I noticed how he is becoming
the sharp-bodied boy he was
when he ran these hills
until he knew them better
than he knew his own father,
who knew them better than
the shape of *his* father's hands.

Then I watched him bend into sleep—
embryo of the king bed,
fetus with dust guts.

On the day of Ed's funeral
he gave me those teeth
"for earrings" he said, "no good
to Ed, or even to me, now."

We buried Ed with manzanita
and bay, those plants
he loved most—our own wish
for *something* to hold forever,
some way to be, in the end,
anything but alone and incomplete.

This dawn I walked
the red mud, looking
for something I could know
would never leave me—
out through the vineyard
where my father tempts life
from dirt to wine in a habit
of seasons stronger than love.
Setting my palms into the mud
at the base of a gnarled vine,
I pressed them together
and whispered "speak."
But the vine's silence just grew
into the silence of the dead
who once tended it.

Then I saw exactly how
it was beautiful—
how it held its world whole
beneath its fog-slick bark,
while the things we ask
to hold us leave us
spent. My handprints in the mud

filled with water and melted
away and my palms—done with prayer,
held out between the earth
and the sky—were empty
and red, and drying into a map.
I flexed them. The rivers widened.

ON THE LAWN AT THE DRUG REHAB CENTER

To my father

Because the wooden lawn statues
here — the bear "whose tail
could be an emerging turd" says Gale,
the squatting monkey, the cow
with taut udders — are all vaguely
obscene, this lawn is not quite
institutional. We sit, half a family
in a circle, Gale, Richie and I
— with our father, dad — groping
awkwardly back to each other.

You ask our ages: we are
older than you thought, much.
You offer us each a small cigar
and ask if we are happy.

The blue smoke turns to water
in my lungs. Gale brings out
the pornographic comics she's working on,
in which her history teacher
meets an embarrassing end.
The teacher's kidnapped—ransom set.
Nobody pays. The ransom is reduced
and reduced again. It would be awful—
ransom demanded and nobody
so much as notices. We laugh.

You say our faces,
the night we came to lock you up,
made a beautiful circle
around you. And then you stop
and I see it coming —"What

do you want from me anyway, you fucking
kidnappers?" I'll tell you. Exactly.

I want you to tell the truth—
our faces were *not* beautiful.
Truth is you fired five shots
and we scattered. Behind the stone
pillar between the vineyard
and the house I thought, that night,
of how you taught us, years ago,
to stand quietly among the vines,
to close our eyes and listen
with our feet to the sound
of the grapes growing. I listened
and I didn't hear them, father.
I heard the words
I'd read on intervention theory—
"Tell the addict how he has
let you down. Have specific
examples ready." Useless.
But we went after you again.

I know there are rooms in the mind
anyone can walk into—
I'm not saying they're any worse
than this strange lawn,
or any better,
but if you want to march
methodically into that complicated
place, I want you
to stand up first, to shake my hand
and say good-bye.

MY FATHER'S FLESH

I know the things I know:
my father's flesh will not
keep him warm much longer.
He cannot say why
he hates it.

The worms are
working their way to his heart.
Every day there are more of them
inside him. They enter
his white arms and leave
their red tracks.

Their red tracks
scorch me when I go to hug him
and a black mouth ruptures
on my forehead. It
will not stop laughing.
I cannot find my hat.
Worms. Mouth. Scorch.

I cannot find my hat.
The mouth laughs and laughs—
uncontrollable as a dog
barking at a fire. I say
"love." The mouth snarls
"fool." I say "but love,
love." My father watches.

For all I can say
I am just a woman
on fire. My father's flesh
cannot keep him warm
enough. I cannot say why
he hates it but I know
the things I know: I am
just a woman, burning.

TO THE MEMORY

of J.S. Bach because on bad nights
I take my three brown dogs to bed
with a box of crackers, which we share
while I sing them their favorite song:

Sheep may safely graze on pasture
when their shepherd guards them well.
Sheep may safely graze on pasture…

I have lived by how this is funny.
I address myself to the dead now.

My body thinks she is the moon—the moon
as remembered against the metal bars
of a bridge whose arc we trust
the more the less we can.

From a distance the cars move to music.
From a distance the world sings back.

My body thinks she is the moon
but she is a clown and I
am all music and unbearably
weighted down. My small dog

on the pillow, upside down,
wiggles her feet, my mean dog
would kill for me, my old dog
cries all night for me to kill her.

Johann Sebastian Bach—
from here I can't speak back.

SUBSTANCE ABUSE TRIAL

He mispronounces you,
the judge, rhyming your first
with your second name,
making you into something
ridiculous: Gillis Willis Mead.

But you stand as still
as they taught you in the army
when you were a young man trying hard
to keep secret what you knew
about how to kill with germs.
As quietly as we used to stand
on the front porch together at dusk
listening for the first cricket of the evening.

Now you stand accused
of wanting to die, of saying so
endlessly, with needles—and the speechless
track marks recording it all.

The evidence is
a red river, mounting.
It wants to carry you
away like an old chair
some fisherman forgot
to take home. And I want
to shout: listen
        —this man
        is my father.
        I love him.

Is there a place
where all those things
that catch in the throat
gather and shape themselves
into something as soft
as the G in Giles
was meant to be pronounced?

Is *that* where you thought
you were going?

TO NOBODY: FEBRUARY 20, 1985

(On the way to K Mart to buy a filing cabinet.)

What I wanted was a solid exchange
of cash for steel, but
the surcharge—that hallucinatory
exchange of pleasantries
that turns existence to the air
around a curtsy—was more
than I could pay
and I kept driving.
The white fields
have a world to themselves,
but human silence needs
a human shelf, so I depended
on the way I knew—
each time I shifted gears—
the team of Swedes
who made my car and, trusting
only that solid connection,
drove. Here at the Stagsfoot
Motel, I'll M.C.
my life tonight. No more
smiles at the register, no more
false currency. Disregard
is a counterfeit word:
the things we choose
to do define us. So,
while I may choose,
one day, to forgive her,
I do not mourn Sarah.
  August 1, 1977.
  Heroin.
  Or Reed.
  June 18, 1978.

O.D.'d.
I do not mourn Paul.
November 15, 1983.
D.O.A.
Or Dad.
Missing.
Twenty-nine days now.

You cowards.

I have snapped the back
of this year in some town
I do not care to know
the name of. Here
at the Stagsfoot
hoof
paw
jaw
breath of mildew
where I'm M.C.,
keeper of the key
to room one-o-one,
I do not even mourn
the voices between my ears
or care
why they cut out.
You cowards.

What I wanted was steel and square.
Cash for gas.
Grease for gears.

AFTER DETOX

I

"For ten days panic will claw your face, then it will be over."

I like the pale light best: the light of dusk
and the light of dawn. And in the hours between—the soft
yellow in the light of closed eyes. On my back,
sometimes I clench them for flashes—like worrying
the red dictionary for words—that don't cut
deep enough. My arms have finally released
my body. My body has fallen back into itself,
fallen into an undisturbed place where nerves
lead nowhere. I think—life. I think—death.
Laundry, I think. Eat. Laundry. Death. Eat.
The light comes softly around curtains; the light
leaves slowly, leaking out around curtains. The sun
is rising and falling. No dying claims my thoughts;
no gem of whisky, no flower of opium
names them. I do my laundry every evening,
walk mechanically down the faded street to where the warm
machines rattle and hum, and the warm soap splashes
behind glass. A life as clean as a bed.
A bed in a room. My hand goes out to touch
a teacup. It is there. Nothing moves in the pure
dim behind my eyes, where thoughts once darted. I wait.
My socks will match. My hair will shine. I like
the pale light best. The light of dusk and the light of dawn.
It seeps around my life slowly. It leaves
without knocking. It has no ending and no beginning,
and all the rest—that other death they call living.

II

"Living"

Everybody in my family has something he must do
to hold us all up; two days after my mother
took me home I had my old job back. I work
at a diner. Luci's Place—with a lot of road traffic
and some regulars. Luci's Place—with sunflowers
between the parking lot and the light green
concrete-block wall; in summer their stems bend
under the huge weight of blossoms. I hide
under grubby clatter; I work at a diner
on the outskirts of town, but it's the green glare
of trees—which hurts my eyes—I died for.

In the morning, sitting in my nightgown by the window,
I watch the light seep around the corners of Glen's Garage.
Yellow, orange, blue. Colors of the rainbow
or the sky rising. Colors on the rusted plates
on the rusted cars. Cars with their toes turned up,
tires sold, fenders missing. Cars from all over, with maps
of stars on the windshields where heads have smashed.

I read stories full of people with descriptions—
some of them have noses that are big, eyes that are small,
skin that is bad, but noses, eyes and skin somebody
has bothered to describe. I try to think of my life in plot.
Bamboozled. But I laugh, for I know that the sunflowers
and the old cars with the pale light at their edges
are all the beauty I'll ever need to hold me up.

I speak softly to the light when its white hands
warm my cheeks. I speak softly to the world,
but I can never explain the way life fades
as it approaches, the way, mid-sentence, I'll realize
it's not me who is speaking, and listen
to the strange words of a strange voice. Or the way
what it is that I'm meant to be doing is always
just on the tip of my tongue. Or why I began
in the northwest quadrant of my forehead,
just above the hairline, and carved, with mother's
dullest knife, the long diagonal line that ends
at the right side of my jaw. Or how the wide red scar
—its shiny translucent skin—turned out
exactly as I wanted. I can never explain,
but it should speak for itself—the map
of a vision, proof that I exist. It's only honest—
to wear your skin as if it were your own.

THE MEMORY

The body refuses to die.
The soul refuses to be stronger.
The memory I cannot fully form
will never fully leave me—
the memory of a man who tried to save me:
vague curve of shoulders and back
disappearing down the playground path
between snowdrifts. Swingchains
on my hands in winter.

Come back—there must be something
you must have forgotten—.

Did he wear a red scarf?
Was he shoeless in the snow?
He had a three day's beard—or, no—
he was clean-shaven. He bent over.
With his warm breath he unfroze
my hands from the swingchains—
not pulling till they were ready.

If only he would tell me now:
What does it mean to let go?

Sometimes a strange feeling comes over me.
My body tingles as if it were alone
with the soul, trying to explain to her
its inability. She understands.
She needs something.

Why is she not complete?
What does she need to be complete?

Ask the present, ask the body. No,
ask the blurred snowdrift darkening, quick—
ask the child on the swingset; she knows.

It was a red scarf.
Yes, and the wind blew it as he bent over
and the knees of his unbelted pants were baggy.
His breath loosened my hands from the chains,
from the swingset. He whispered
"let go."

Then he turned and walked sadly
down the playground path and suddenly,
in the tired curve of a back,
my body recognized itself.

Nothing more. Nothing forgotten.

It seems wrong—
the way the body refuses to die.
It seems wrong—
the way the soul refuses to be stronger.

There should have been something more.
A binding word perhaps—*body, sorrow*—
or a parting glance dissolving—
too late, too late, too late.

But now, at least, there is nothing
between me and my soul but myself.

TO THE BODY

I don't know how to speak to you.
I have tried and tried, but I don't
know how to answer.

I gave you tide pools for your feet,
salt on wind for your lips
and the sound of waves for your ears:

Nothing.

I made you stare through the arch of a window
where Simon left his body hanging:
Nothing, not a tremor.

I tried the junkie's twilight sleep,
but you would not come with me. I climbed
the stairs in a house by the sea.

Climbed past the porthole on the landing,
the tailless lizard in the corner,
and let the stranger's hands massage you.

I forgot myself and let her have you.
These things I did for you because of what I know:
there is no easy truce of words forthcoming.

And you just pushed the clear tears out—
they dripped down the bench to the carpet—
they kept on coming—as if I'd understand.

As if I'd understand or could go with you.

TWO

SPARROW, MY SPARROW

The voice that loves me best when I am dreaming
comes from every corner of the circle of my sleep
speaking in the sound of my own drowning.
She says *the body's just a habit getting old,*
a crystal turning on a nerve of ancient longing.
She says *I will teach you how to be with yourself*
always, she says *we do not live in the same world.*

All this is just an allegory for the truth.
Truth is, I cannot speak
the voice that I've been dreaming.
Truth is, the slate sky darkens,
clouds of sparrows heave in the wind,
the trees are massed with sparrows screaming
and the fields are dotted with them.
The birds are bracing themselves. The birds
are frenzied by something about to happen.

Truth is, I have my feet on the slimy banks.
I look for my face in the murk-green river
and the water's surface does not change.

But I hear myself in the screech of sparrows
and am panicked by something about to happen.

Slate sky—darkened; sound in wind:
I enter this world like myself as a prayer.
I enter this world as myself.
I cannot help myself.

What is a prayer but a song of longing
turning on the thread of its own history?

I feel myself loved by a voice in the wind—
I cover my ears with my palms.
The whole world rocks and still
the cold green river does not spill.

MAPPING THE MIND

One thing I know for certain—
there's a slow green river
I've been living by.

Not the banks: in their green-gold light
there's a message I can't read.

Not the carp those fishermen
keep leaving on the shore—
though because I know raccoons
have been eating carp eyes in the night
my life must be imperceptibly changed.

No. Not the banks, not the carp—
and not the vine-tangled trees.
I do not love them—though I love
how the river reflects them.

This green line, then, will stand
for the river and the river
running through me.

Now, what will the banks be?
I must marry them to me.
A river needs banks or it has no course.

What will the banks be,
and how will I know when I have found them?

And when I have drawn them in, then,
where will my soul be—

who must surely be returning
else she would have taken me with her.

Wouldn't she?

She must surely be returning.

I can draw a solitary bird
circling her reflection in the river.

Now let her enter.

IN NEED OF A WORLD

Who wouldn't want a life
made real by the passage of time
or a world, at least,
made real by the mind. Something
solid and outer, though connected.

Who wouldn't want to know
for certain how to get there?

I'd like to tell you simply
how I passed this day putting tomatoes up,
or how I tied a stern cicada to a string
so I could feel the gentle tug
its flying in frantic circles made.

I'd like to show you the red
worm-shaped burn on my wrist
and in this way claim myself.

Instead I slip out of my every day—
away into the distant and lulling sound
of "once-upon-a-time-there-was-a-woman."

Will I ever find that perfect stance
of soul and mind from which sparks
a self uttering itself?
I'm always slipping between rows of corn—
through the field that rises toward this ridge
from which I like the houses for their smallness.

Here I lean against a Honey Locust,
feathery tree with its three-inch thorns,
and watch sagging strands of barbed wire
sway slightly in the wind—the clump
of brown fur hanging there, waving.

I watch the field of drying corn beyond,
and beyond that the soccer field
and rows of clean-lined condos.
I wait for the yellow light to flick on
in the white church across the valley.

Will I ever learn the way to love
the ordinary things I love to look at?

I'm always slipping away
between rows of corn, climbing
toward this ridge to think,
when really what I want is a ridge
or a lonely field on the edge of the world
of the mind. A place from which to speak
honestly to that man on the porch, a way
to greet the children who are swinging
on the edge of dusk behind chain-link fences.

But always it's either I or world.
World or I.

And when it's I, I'm dreaming
on a quiet ridge that the tomatoes
ripened and, though I was missing,

a woman put an apron on and canned them.
And when it's world, it pushes me back
towards that madness of the soul
which is not a field, nor a ridge, nor a way.

BEGIN WHERE WE ALL KNOW WHICH
AND WHERE WE ARE

I

Carquinez, Dumbarton, Benicia and Bay

It begins with the world and its many bridges
receding, and how you make a song to hold it,
how you sing out loud for all you're worth—
Carquinez, Dumbarton, Benicia and Bay—and how
then even the song goes off beyond static.

And you know that it's the body's story rising
up to meet you, here where you're wrong in life,
so you sweep dead bugs from the window ledge
with the knife edge of your hand just to see the arc
your arm makes, and feel the powdered wings if you can.

But still there's just a literal numbness spreading
so you try to think where you lost your foothold,
but you can't cover the distance back, or out
to where the red wing flickers in the air
on the dull mat of sky, that faded square.

And you know that elsewhere there's another body
fallen, and it's the body of your own dismay
in a bright and drizzly season under thunder,
against the dark face of a cliff, and you think
perhaps the way back in would be to go there.

And when you get there the place has changed some:
you note the branches and the good sun shining,
how the yellow star thistles make a field; you note
the many Ceanothus in the Ceanothus bush,
you the looker looking—and never arriving.

So you stay with that thought for as long as you can,
yo-yoing out to the brim and back in, back
to where you began, where you fed your dogs
which was a prayer for the world to begin, for the body
to mention herself: *here, here, I'm over here.*

But she isn't stirring so you try the memory:
the middle of Iowa, the middle of winter, the middle
of the night, snow on the baseball field, moonlight on it,
how it came to you: so *this* is the world. You
remember too how it was gone by morning.

The quail are scruffing in the underbrush,
you think that's got to do with why you're here—
but it isn't any good and it's taken everything
you have to trust it, and meanwhile you're
just waiting and it gets to be a long time.

II

The Body's Story Rising

If you want to tell the story of what happens
when sound waves don't share a common center
you could begin with how, in 1842,
Christian Johan Doppler loaded a flatcar
with fifteen professional trumpeters
and rolled them by a stationary listener.

You could begin with the image of a trumpet
in sunlight, the sound of a symphony

over the sound of wheel on rail, steel
on steel. However you begin, however much
you want to keep them reading, it will all return,
in the end, to where you started, what you know.

The sound, say, of an ambulance missing the driveway.
Try mentioning the cottonwood swaying in the night—
leaving out the window too small to crawl through—
and pretty soon you'll see what the cottonwood's for,
it's there because you need to tell what happened,
you need to keep them long enough to hurt them.

Sooner or later, you'll get to the ambulance—
and the man in the house who keeps beating the woman.
The worst part then will be your refusal
to stop telling it. The worst part will be
their refusal to read on. The worst part
is the way you need to hurt them.

You thought the words arriving is what kept you,
but suddenly you're crazy with the image
on the edge, how it's got to be maintained, how
it's the last place there is for those who live there—
and you start with caution, you start
with naked women running on the beach.

You describe the waves and the pretty sky,
you say the sun is setting, justify the lie,
because you know you're going to bring the men in,
you know it's about soldiers slashing the women
from behind as they are running, you know
and so you promise sex from the beginning.

And before you know it, before they know it,
you've moved from the dream to the truth
about how some of the women enter the water
bleeding, about what happened to the ones
who never get there. Who are you losing?
Some of us enter the water bleeding.

We swim and they follow. We wake in prison
because we do not know whose side we're on.
We're the one who leads the keeper to the cell.
The one who lets him in, and the woman
with the dead face lying there, her too.
We know the significance of her henna hair.

We know it will happen before he rapes her,
how the slick of semen on her crotch
matches exactly the glaze on her eyes, body
like a board—you know the feeling? Body
as the lie you live by, a pronoun
as a hundred pounds of meat in search of meaning.

You end with the image of the bruise he made,
how she jabs it just to keep it, how it's
how she holds her place, how you hold your place.
This is the story of twenty-one years spent
looking for a place to put my hands, a way
to be here, practicing the posture of erasure.

There are whole days I spend with music.
Afternoons made of my need to go there.
Just that now, and the image of a bruise,
its many paths receding—the body as bruise,
the bruise as the story, and the story
as the answer to not being here.

A NOTE ON THE PRESENT STATE OF THE FUTURE

Just when he's finally buttering her a roll
it will occur to me, these aren't
rock trucks I've been hearing, not

their routine squall as they near the hairpin
and see the cliff approaching. Same rumble
but trucks going up. I'll close the book

and realize it's fire trucks—
sirens off for the long heave
through the country. And when the lights go out

I'll know: you *could* gather rocks
in this kind of moonlight, you could
do it just to do it and be glad.

When I call the man at P G & E he'll say
my power's out, they're getting to it, and
now that you ask, yes, there *is* a fire

and when I call the man at Forestry
he'll be a recording concerning the need
for permits and inspection of burning sites,

ending with a number for Forestry 2,
who will tell me my power's out. I
won't ask him to come and spend the night,

won't even tell him how I know—
when this hill goes up in flames
it goes, nothing left of this house

eight years ago but some concrete steps.
Instead, I'll just say thanks, and try
to dump this all in one final guffaw

and run—like thinking about electricity
and fire and how when transformers blow it looks
and sounds like the Fourth of July. Meanwhile, I'm

working by candlelight on a description
of fire, taking comfort in the notion
of the poverty of description, doodling

in the margins—stairs going down, which is
as far as my not-so-famous talent takes me:
There's a pit at the end of every thought

and it wants me like Br'er Rabbit's
anything. Anything. For example,
the thought of what I cannot do—the one

about two women, one who is *other*
and the other, who is beaten,—and the pit
saying choose. Or a thought for a poem that ends

with the speaker wondering briefly
why she's still alone, then reopening the novel
at the spot where a man hands a woman a roll,

and how she will read by the light of the moon,
and how then she will read by the approaching fire,—
the whole thing insisting on closure now,

when somewhere there's still an image
on the loose—the one that contains the moment
at which she might say *might*—say *yes*, say *no*.

TO VINCENT VAN GOGH
OF THE HOUSE HE PAINTED
IN 1890, THE YEAR OF HIS DEATH

This evening my valley has the colors
of your "House at Auvers"—your colors,
my colors now. Fog smudges up from the bay
and is lost in the blue-green fields—
it's the color of the lake through mist, color
of the smoke from five damp trash fires
which drifts up towards elsewhere, taking
its time. This is the color you gave
your sky, this is the color you gave
your house. The greens I see are the ones *you* chose
for roof and shrubs and shutters, and I—
in my red flannel shirt—could be
the flame of poppies you put in the corner.

Except that nothing human strays there—
there is no sign of human life at all.

I have come from planting blackberries,
sunflowers and cabbages—planting them
to hold me here a while longer,
in this house overlooking the valley.

The valley is fading in dusk and warm rain.

All the houses are dropping away. They are leaving
too fast. What if we never have our moment?

And what if it's all there—in your painting—
what if there *is* no missing gesture? What

if a shovel left by the gate would not have done,
if putting it there could not have saved you?

And if it's *not* the absence in your windows
of a frail hand pulling curtains back,
of a face, half-shadowed, looking toward you—
then it must be that you knew too well
just how to make the sagging woodshed lovely.

The world is still much larger than itself.
The world is still unbearable or small:
greens, blues, flame of poppies, smoke
rising up toward elsewhere—taking its time.

BACH, WINTER

Bach must have known—how
something flutters away when you turn
to face the face you caught sideways
in a mirror, in a hall, at dusk—

and how the smell of apples in a bowl
can stop the heart for an instant,
between sink and stove,
in the dead of winter when stars

of ice have spread across the windows
and everything is perfectly still
until you catch the sound of something
lost and shy beating its wings.

And then: music.

PARADISE CONSISTS OF FORTY-NINE ROTATING SPHERES

paradise gave me these legs
   for spinning
weep and pray and be joyful
paradise gave me these legs
    to weep and pray and be joyful

when I have fixed each corner
    p l i é relevé spin
I start the silky spokes
       p l i é relevé spin

paradise gave me these legs
    to weep and pray
              I am joyful

    youthful youthful
       paradise gave me these legs
so I spin
    black nights
      blue days
           p l i é relevé spin
my web against the sky

    a perfect circle shakes the stars
mine's a pure imitation
    sung from planets of memory
      spun from threads of dreams
weep and pray and be joyful

    paradise gave me these legs
that's all I need to know
paradise gave me these legs
    for spinning
I have spun
forty-nine webs of silken threads
    my window to the sky

LAGUARDIA, THE STORY

I

A man in the clot of colors—which are people—
is holding a naked iris, is watching
the long line of faces unloading.

He holds the flower up to his chest, then
down at a tilt to his side—in one hand
behind his back makes a surprise.

He runs through his posture
now and again. He uses
one shoe at a time for standing.

The long line of faces—its trickle and blurt—
hurts me. He is watching for her face.

She must have sat at the back of the plane—
a seven-forty-seven: she's been smoking.
Perhaps something has happened that matters.
Perhaps what has happened is nothing—
but the face that arrives is never
the face that left us. Remember that.

I want to rest my head on his back,
on his blue flannel shirt. I imagine
her face which must arrive. I imagine
that she must not disappoint him.

Will I know her before he sees her?
What does their story mean to me?

I used to walk through Kensington Gardens
every morning on my way to school
that winter we lived at Lancaster Gate.
This is a story too—does it have meaning,
is it about something that matters—does it
tell how the branches aged the white sky?

Is its secret in the fog or the red sun rising,
in the ducks on the Serpentine as seen
through a layer of mist—can it explain
why my mother whimpered in her sleep that year?

In the frame story she walks off last,
sees the flower—hands up for a moment
for *surprise* before she takes it.

She gives him a small kiss and they head off
arm in arm down the long hall
happily, until I can no longer see them.

This is the story as I saw it happen.
The story as I told it.

In their second story he waits with the iris
long after she doesn't arrive—
but for some other reason than for
so-I-can-save-him: she has been delayed—
perhaps by something inconsequential,
we don't know yet, but in the second story

she does not arrive. This is the story
as I imagine it—the story that exists.

Is there any other possible story?

Walking home from school in the afternoons
I'd stop and sit by the Serpentine
and rub my fingers on the curbstone.
I loved the raw circles I made in their tips—
symmetrical and red as the skin
under the popped bubble of a blister.

Is there any other story possible?
Who must I be to make her exist?

II

I am stuck in the middle of the story,
not knowing if she will arrive.
I saw her face, this makes no difference—
there is a man at LaGuardia
holding an iris. When I think of it
I cannot stop fearing for him.

How do you unlock a story? How
do you recognize the image—'
the one that might change you?

If I put in the part about my mother
and step-father fighting, if I describe
—perfectly—his body in action,
his shadow on the wall behind him,
or add the bit about it all boiling down
to inquisitions in the rational morning—as in
whose dark anus holds the safe-box key—
will we have a story with a meaning?

There is a way to discover a truth
about anything you want to know.

I imagine there's a way to know what's real.

Listen—I walked through an empty park
every morning on my way to school
and knew that it was good to be human.

Some nights I make a killer pot of coffee—
I put on the music that I love,
and dance. Sometimes I dance for hours.

Go to your phonograph. Put on
Brandenburg Concerto Number Six.

This is about something very hard.
—This is about trying to live with that music
playing in the back of your mind.

—About trying to live in a world
with that kind of music.

THREE

BETWEEN SELF AND CENTURY

This is the century of the one lost shoe
at the side of the highway, century
of the old shoe curled back at the toe,
sole split, the usual mud-streaked heel.

This is the century of the big black oak
at the far end of this field of gold,
oak blurred by the air between us—
looking like a cloud of smoke, black
against the white smoke that is the sky.

* * *

I wanted to be the girl doing leg-lifts
in front of the evening news, the one
who's up on current events, but countries
I don't recognize the names of keep falling
and I'm between field and highway with the names
of those countries burning into my skull.

I'm the one who's always fasting
as if God would then come in,
the one with twigs snarled in her hair
watching a penful of pigs.
They lie in the mud shitting themselves
and squinting at me. I love them
because nothing can do *pig* as well as pig
and I am lost and do not know who I am, or if
life has anything to do with prayer.

* * *

The man who called me yellow-bird
had nothing to do with me.
He called me that because *he* wanted to fly
just as my sister called me limbs
so she would not have to love me.

But they had nothing to do with me.

There ought to be an image around here somewhere
with its back pushed up snug against that cloud,
an image to hold the world up, refusing
to shrug, refusing, even, to weep.

But this is the century of the old shoe.

* * *

There must have been something I loved once.
Some thing I made bright.

I think of the yellow curtains I made
for the kitchen of a small brown house.
A house that sat on the edge of a river.
Every morning my hands swept them open.
Every evening I closed them again.

Yes, it was the yellow checked curtains I made
so carefully—crooked to match the crooked house.

I must still be the woman who pulled curtains back.
I must be the road back into myself.

There must be something there. I loved
the motion of hands letting light in,
my own hands sweeping curtains back,
arching across the arc of the morning,
two white doves at the window, looking out
and the tide of light pouring in.

THE ARGUMENT AGAINST US

The line of a man's neck, bent
over welding, torchlight breaking
shadows on his face, hands cracked
into a parched map of fields he has woken—
the gods wanted us.

Think of their patient preparation:
the creature who left the rocking waves behind,
crawling up on some beach, the sun
suddenly becoming clear. Small thing
abandoning water for air, crooked body
not quite fit for either world, but the one
that finally made it. Think of all the others.

Much later, spine uncurls, jaw pulls back, brow-bone
recedes, and as day breaks over the dry plain
a rebellious boy takes an upright step
where primitive birds are shrieking above him.

He did it for nothing. He did it
against all odds. Bone of wrist, twist
of tooth, angel of atoms—an infinity
of courage sorted into fact
against the shining backdrop of the world.

The line of one man's neck, bent—
torchlight breaking shadows on his face.

There was a creature who left the waves behind
and a naked child on a windy plain:
when the atom rips out into our only world
and we're carried away on a wave of hot wind
I will love them no less: they are just how much
the gods wanted us.

FOR ALEX AT THE GLADMAN MEMORIAL HOSPITAL

Because he is kicking and knows
he's not going to make it, Alex
is in love with what he's painting.

He's got the mountain in, and the
mountain-and-sky-in-the-lake, is saving
all of tomorrow for the upper sky, because

"With that you got to take your time."
There's something broken, something
whole in how he says it, and something

he's working on mending, like
how the black line of shore runs
between mountains, like

knowing that whatever we're wanting
is not far from here—no farther, maybe,
than the fix he'll get to fix it when they

throw up their hands at his mum pastorals
and boot him out. He doesn't know
shit from you-know-what about shoes

but he's familiar with the facts upstream,
knows the paint on the Golden Gate
is poisonous and that here he wants

to use blues that refer to each other—
as in lake-blue mountain and what's
going to be the mountain-blue sky when

and if he gets there. He wants
to agree with his body. He
wants to know if it's a bad gene,

or if it's got to do with signs
and the times—with the century
writ small enough to piss on.

But even if we *are* the scene
behind this scene, I'm still not going
to leave you with that squint from a distance

through some gritty air where bridge
and sandblaster meet as something like
a pale cloud of golden mist and the bay

below calm as a lily, but gray—
or with *gold close the mountain*
and part ways with syntax though

they're a fix of sorts. No, if you
follow this road as far as you can,
you will arrive at a blotch, which,

if it's in the foreground, recommends
itself in the shade and the shape
of a bird, and, if it's in the background,

desires to desire to depict miles
of bay-blue sky, by Alex. Alex—
wrapped in a blanket, a man describing

a painting, clumsily describing
his many careful brushstrokes, his
long reach out toward something true—

without turning elsewhere, which is
indebtedness, which is annihilation
when we can call it anything we want.

THE MAN IN THE POETRY LOUNGE

at Berkeley is reading English
pastoral poetry with passive
abandon, chewing his thumbnail
aggressively. He wants

to see grass, he wants to
BE grass so badly he can
almost smell it. Outside,
they are cutting the grass—

the man and the mower—they are
dressing and keeping the garden.
They are not far enough away
from my hayfever, but the man

reading pastorals is off—
zeroing in on calmer places.
Have the birds arrived yet?
Have the larks and nightingales

made their appearance? I would like
to ask him to let me know
when he gets to the birds. I would like
to concentrate then and there, and lose

what I have read about Flanders
and Picardy and the trenches of WW I:
the larks appearing around the time
of stand-to in the morning,

the nightingales showing up
by stand-to at night. I would like never

to have learned that they were there.
But instead, because my nose is running,

my eyes are getting smaller by the minute,
and I'm edgy, I'll ask him sweetly
if he's bothered at home
by bedbugs, rats, or lice,

and justify the question with an explanation:
I myself am bothered by fleas.
This is why I keep scratching—
which act I hope he does not find

distracting because, really,
who am I to ruin his birds.
I who cannot, as you have seen,
follow those trenches to their

logical conclusion. Instead, I too
have searched long, and found
that in the gentle arc
of a pig's back there really is

a thought to calm the thinker—
if, that is, the pig be tame.
I want to know if this man
loves what he is reading—

and if he loves it enough
in what way it will change him.
Are we onto something real now
or is this all about planting

a false goose in front of the moon?
Do the iambs soothe him? Is he
big on true rhyme and false conclusion,
the sonic hanky—you wipe your eyes

you blow your nose. Which I will
have to leave this room to do.
But not before I've resisted
coming right out and asking

if he's fulfilling the requirements
of heart or mind, and asked instead
what it's my true right to know
(involving, as it does, the heat

of concentration, the problem
of public safety, as in MY safety):
if his shirt, which I'll begin
by calling handsome, has passed

the requirements of the Flammable
Fabrics Act. Then I'll
step out and blow my nose,
at which point I might as well wander

back on down toward Cody's and try
to receive the world, browsing
and scratching in the poetry section,
after buying a paper poppy for a dollar—

the one you didn't want to know was coming—
the Flanders—from a veteran of foreign wars

at Telegraph and Durant—not,
of course, looking at his left leg—

because I can't.
Because it isn't there.

THE CASE OF THE MISPLACED CAPTION

You can take it back now, not
as in beginning *in medias res*,
but as in your desire for a plot—

because if what you want to know
is that on January 17 of some
new year Toyotas went on sale

in Sacramento, where there was
a subplot involving the San
Francisco dealer, and I

saw the dentist, nine a.m.,
perfect teeth, and war, what?
broke out? having repercussions

throughout the economy, the immediate
universe, our teeth, our Toyotas, our
ability to keep both body and soul,

then I offer you this:
she looks into the camera
out at all America and says

*I'm sure he'll come back, he's
a good soldier*. Listen.
Listen to it. The

marriage is over folks.
Read it in *Redbook*, read it
in *McCall's*, read it at the dentist:

A noted royal biographer
creates a correspondence
that takes us inside

the hearts and minds of
Charles and Diana.
Or, seen the other way—

New York Times best seller
number eleven, *The Secret*
Diary of Laura Palmer:

put it on your night-stand
put it in your hand, your head,
put yourself in the story—

eight ninety-five, which is
not nine, but rather the marriage
of psychology and economics

at some small expense to small us.
And then there's what we're down to—
ABC pulls episode of spy show:

"It's so close to what's going on
we didn't want to run it, it
could scare the hell out of people."

Lady, you might not want him back,
and it's not your fault, but
this isn't the chapter

where the witch gets roasted—no trail
of crumbs in this forest, just you
and how you *really*

might not want him back, not
alive, that is, and that
when I tell you just how he

held the gun, aimed the camera,
made the lens, wrote the story,
sold the magazine, or mention

that he went down with his
arms around his child,
we've reached the six-he level

of pronoun saturation, meaning
you can either be a good
soldier and put this down

or continue on into *who
couldn't he be?* You see
there's an agenda

under the agenda, having
to do with how both *taken*
and *image* reside

in the case of the hero's
photo, having to do
with the universal rights of man,—

and it moves to a logic that goes
like this: *In the event*
of multiple losses resulting

from the same accident
only one amount is payable—
the largest amount applicable,

which is what the dead
say to the living in the moment
before the gun goes off:

you have the right to silence,
you have the right to the ashes
on your hands, the ashes

that are your hands. Christ,
your rights, your vote, your
recycle bins, your desire

for a plot. You
can take them back. This
is my body, I offer it

to the dead now. Let the
stars go on with their stories.

It was love that led me here.

IN THE PARKING LOT AT THE JUNIOR COLLEGE ON THE EVE OF A PRESIDENTIAL ELECTION

I've been sitting in this parking lot
for a long time—thinking
about nothing. The bumper sticker
on the car next to mine reads
BORN TO SHOP, and makes me wonder
why I can't laugh too—why I
can't laugh with the best of us.

There's a small New Testament,
bound in calf, on my dashboard—
someone I love has died and left me
with it, a cryptic trail guide
to some foreign land.

Once upon a time there was
a man named Abraham. (At first
he seemed like an ordinary man.)

He begat Isaac who begat
Jacob who begat Judah and his brethren.
Then Perez and Zerah of Tamar.

And the song on a radio blaring past—
    Talking about the splendour
    of the Hoover Factory—
    know that you'd agree
    if you had seen it too.

Hezron, Ram, Amminadab.
Nahshon, Salmon, Boaz of Rahab,
Obed, Jesse and David the King…

Five miles out of London
on the Western Avenue—
must have been a wonder
when it was brand new.

Manasseh, Amon, Josiah, Jechoniah—
Jechoniah of the time
of the carrying away to Babylon.

And what might there be for us
now that Babylon has been blown
all the way to Coventry?

What might there be now for us?
Some small prayer—some bold
giving over of what remains?

And Jechoniah begat Shealtiel
who begat Zerubbabel.

I, like you, am tired
of names. There are so many
names, and we are so impatient.
We are so important!

Yesterday my fat student Marty
announced that his favorite pastime
was hanging out at McDonald's.
The whole class laughed
as if they have always known
the world was about to end.

They are young enough
to have known this
for the whole of their lives.

And Joseph the husband of Mary
of whom was born Jesus,
who is called Christ.

But who must have been,
after all, just a man.
Right?

Abraham. We could, perhaps,
have an Abraham among us.
And if it were possible
to wait for forty-two lifetimes
we might have been able
to come to something better.

Abraham. Abraham—
I'm talking about the wonder.

DELPHI, COMING AROUND THE CORNER

Delphi, coming around the corner of the house,
one shoe on foot, one shoe in hand, says
he thought the dog shit was just a shadow.

This has happened before.
He scrapes it off on my door stoop, off
to the side, we wait for rain.

Meanwhile, my idea of an afternoon
is a couple of dogs chewing cow toes
in my bed—and me, and Delphi,

whom I love. Delphi, who
cannot read or write. Sometimes
I try to teach him—goes like this:

This is my Oil of Olay, T.M., this
is my shell-pink polish, also T.M.ed,
and these are the little shrimps that are my toes.

Later I try again. *This is the other*
side of the story, I say,
picking up the book and quoting:

"Writing is that (dot dot dot) space
where all identity is lost, starting with the
(dot dot dot) identity of the body writing."

Unquote, I say, adding a footnote[1]
just in case. Delphi puts the book
on the floor. Later I try again.

---

1.   Roland Barthes, *Image—Music—Text*, trans. Stephen Heath
     (New York: Hill and Wang, 1977), p.142

This is my poem for you, I say,
this is the place where I can't,
for a song, put the song in. So I sing it.

Delphi sings harmony, the dogs stop chewing.
Delphi knows the end to every story,
his literal, illiterate eyelids fluttering shut.

PASSING A TRUCK FULL OF CHICKENS AT NIGHT ON HIGHWAY EIGHTY

What struck me first was their panic.

Some were pulled by the wind from moving
to the ends of the stacked cages,
some had their heads blown through the bars—

and could not get them in again.
Some hung there like that—dead—
their own feathers blowing, clotting

in their faces. Then
I saw the one that made me slow some—
I lingered there beside her for five miles.

She had pushed her head through the space
between bars—to get a better view.
She had the look of a dog in the back

of a pickup, that eager look of a dog
who knows she's being taken along.
She craned her neck.

She looked around, watched me, then
strained to see over the car—strained
to see what happened beyond.

That is the chicken I want to be.

HOUSE OF POURED-OUT WATERS

For Parry and for Whit —
For my mother

Do the bones cast out their fire?
  —Theodore Roethke, "The Lost Son"

1

TO BREAK THE SPELL IS TO INVITE CHAOS INTO THE UNIVERSE

It would be easier
if I did not exist—

but I did. It would be
easier if there were

nothing left, but there is—
mementos weeded down to

how to miss the out-juttings
below the cliff, ocean

behind all the doors and windows.
Ocean,—and the watery sky.

On the cliff-face the swallow
is making her home of mud and feathers.

Out of mud and feathers
she makes a home.

Earth or music?

The music as the earth: just so:
The horizon beyond the horizon—.

THE FUTURE

As a child, who you were
was located in the future—

right? Now where is
your existence. In

there were dogs—
then we buried them?

Berries, so we put them
in jars? There were

guns, so we fired them
at one another, or didn't——.

Just as the scene was predicted?
Just as the act was forewritten?

RATHER

Rather, we must begin
way before here. To believe
is not so easy. *Paragraph*
after paragraph of rain
was the right thing.

There are children standing
like numb pigeons
in every paragraph—
just watching us.

See, they were not bees at all.
Instead—we are responsible for them.

We said, *sunlit passages*
we can't describe, we said,
blackout. We said,
put out the fiasco.

They said, *we are the fiasco.*

We never said *children* once.

They stood in the heavy downpour,
paragraph after paragraph,

their true mittens hanging from their sleeves—
little red embassies.

AND ALL THESE THINGS ARE SO

If the trees are alive
and I am alive,
if the trees are blazing,

and the seagull—flying
between the grass and sun—
makes a shadow,

if the sky startles me,
if my soul is listening, waiting
for something to fly

from the bony cage of my hands—
then how can it be,
how *can* it be, that when I raise them

and make the motions of blossoming
they are empty?

LACK, THE OWL

Look early, look late.
Look up to fate—
magnify the moment.

Get the gist of it—
magnify the gist of it.—
Where the owl complains.

The owl in the night, complaining.
Who said he speaks to you?
Who said he speaks into night?

Who said he complains.
Define an act of betrayal?
Define an act of faith.

Magnify the moment.
Too much like a wing?
Too much like a shadow?

Too much like fate.—
Exercise the owl sound.
Repel doubt.

Too early. Too late.

THE WORLD

remaining central, there is
some knowledge we do not
debate: a child is born

to his body the day he is
born, for example, or
the sky's felt time

seems like mourning:
the grasshoppers are anonymous
to the anonymous, the birds

are always at attendance.
There comes a moment
when you see as the crow sees:

the body as slaughterhouse,
as beggar—in the long grass, kneeling.

BUT WHAT IF, AS IS

often the case, it takes
months, years even, for that
specific tree to finish
falling, and furthermore

all during that time
lots of birds nest
in that tree, and the tree
and the birds call *each other*

into existence, mutually,—
meaning what if we really
aren't the center of
our spectacularly uncentered

universe but, rather, the tree,
the sound of it falling is what
calls us forth, and then here it is,
taking months, years even—

beginning with its creaking
in the *whispering wind,* working
up to the tiniest of crackings—
and then another patient waiting

for the song of eleven strong
rains, a magic number of fogs
and a certain added heaviness
of moss, until finally, and right

between two of the smallest
units of time (the size of which
of course do not exist, yet are
hauled back now for this occasion

from the land where a duck set out
across a pond and was left
in eternal exhaustion to his own
personal so-close-but-yet-so-far)

what if, that is, it's months
before the split tree splits
a little farther (twice as far,
exactly say, as the first split)

and it does this splitting almost
soundlessly, save for a branch
that hits its neighbor's branch,
sounding like a distant .22,

and what if the *decisive* crack
will come in a future emptied
completely of the likes of us
(*by* the very likes of us)

yet, still, I *am* here now, near that
aforementioned and graceless
shifting, and it takes me
back to the guns of my childhood—

and what if I want *that* to count,
that little crack, so that the memory
now, and therefore the childhood,
are called with me into existence,

meaning back into existence,
and another memory tags along,
for it is a part of that same
childhood, the memory of imagining

a tree and a forest in order to give
some life to a question—couldn't it
all add up, the trees, the moss,
the puny cracking, to me,—

existing, every atom of me,
so that I might have this chance
to ask you (who are a problem
for another day) what brand

of confusion it would take
for what manner of pervert to ask
that particular question
of a potentially invisible child?

LACK, THE MEMORY

Remember the door?
　　I remember the door.

Remember the door and the wall.
　　I remember the wall.

The wall and the Smith and Wesson?
　　The hand blackened by gunpowder.

I remember the weeping.
　　And I remember the door.

But most of all there were iris.
　　Inside and outside.

And amaryllis in the kitchen.
　　The door—left open for the cat.

Left open for the rain.
　　And the ghosts passing through.

Remember the hinges?
　　I remember the door and the hinges.

Remember the sky?
　　And the ragged clouds within.

Think of the worlds within them.
    I remember the one world.

From before or after?
    From before.

From before the gunpowder?
    From before.

So what was the last thing?
    A face—cleansed by grief.

A face, cleansed by grief, in a dream.

THE ANIMAL MESSENGER

The loon call happens
on the marsh now, the marsh
rainbowed with oil—colors

of a chosen landscape,
purples and greens against
the tans and grays of fall

falling into winter.
The loon call happens and happens—
ripples outward, colorless

and shocked, and nowhere
meeting with a love of life
to make it certain.

TALKING TO YOU

*

Night and I'm a chromosome,
spinning.
Rats chew the floorboards.

Day, and I defect.
Roots pushing through the foundation—
ivy, some leaves too, under
my desk in the basement.

Sunlight stutters into this world
bringing another world with it.——

But light's just a question
I'm living through—
banner for the yellow bird,
white flag for the backward word.

Lots of work to be done here. I'm
making flypaper out of history.
——Personal *and* cultural.
——Remember that.

Daylight changes all the answers.
Daylight tries to.

Bars on the window.
Dog on the desk looks through them.
Sometimes she barks, a disintegration
of its own kind—but she loves me.

*

When I get through with drinking
maybe I'll tell you how
sun's a shattering I held onto,
maybe say it some way
you can make use of, maybe.

—Meanwhile, bed's the place
I go home to, and the eerie light
called daylight and the weaker light
that makes the night a vision.

How about *you* tell *me* a story?

Make it to do with the fate of the earth,
start with the world's beginning.
Maybe you could mention
my name—or just say *Julie.*

Then say it's the same
for how I love her.

—The god that is in me
is the god that is in her.

Where do *you* go home to?

*

Lots of work to be done here.
Have you noticed?

My father is a brilliant drunk.
Mutters to himself loudly,
and in public. At best.

I saw my mother laugh once—
most everybody else missed it,
but I say I saw it and I saw.

I myself wanted to live here.
With you.
Sane as a monkey
with someplace to go.

I've done my share of sweeping,
but am erratic.
And unforgivable.

This much I know:
If you start with loss
you go nowhere, and if
you start with nowhere
you start here.

The visions of the day return
as the visions of the night.
And stay.

Call me.

*

Meanwhile, phone unplugged
with a motion as fell
and unspecific as moonlight—
means *you* that is.

When I get through with drinking,
when I get through with thinking,
going to lay this body down—
sleep like something you might get.

Did I say that there's a god
within me?

And if I did, in what
dark corner of your mind
did you then tuck me?

The more I seek the source
of this divinity,
farther I get from time,
farther *you* are from mine.

Where *do* you go home to?

Do you miss me?

*

Because you'll never guess
this rage is love—
I have to tell you:
One glance and I'm with you—
want to dance?

In this way we'll begin
another story,
and it has another side:
One false move and

Damn straight I know
where I'm going.

You should throw your life away
and try it.

*

This is my only story.
I wouldn't trade it
for anything.

Not for a thing.

Do you hear me?
Do you understand?

Daylight resembles the day.
I resemble the sky.
I resemble a glass of water.

I do not think we choose—

night, and I'm a chromosome,
spinning. Days it deepens—

hair plastered to my forehead.
In the end, all I wanted to say
was this: *marrow deep,*
Sweet Jesus how I'm singing.

You should peel your skin off
and hear me.

2

SEVERAL SCENES IN SEARCH OF THE SAME EXPLOSION

+
What I want is
for them to say, to be
able to say, "They
wept well, they sang."

Of us all, and
whoever *they* will be,
in whatever language
speaking: "From

antiquity to their
brooding capsize,
they sang well—*duende*
in their fists, fire

in their feet, dust
of glass in their veins."

+
River mud between my toes
and I can tell you this:
the four dogs have
their four pure joys—

mud on their whiskers,
slime to their knees.
Milk-Bones in my pockets,
kennel up on the

dark of my tongue,
and I save it—though the
house behind the brambles
wants me. *Because*

the house behind
the brambles wants me.
Leon, in prison,
made the plaque that's

hanging in the kitchen:
Home, Sweet Home—
etched on mirror,
brambles of roses

and roses wreathed
around the centered words.

+
Clapboard, sheets on the line—
just what I want, just as
Leon, out now, wants me
to believe his hand,

half-raised again in anger,
can be lowered—*half*
raised: moment erased
by moment. Half

believing: mind
erased by the mind.
True sheets snapping
behind me now,

not like gunshot, but
like gunshot muffled
by the mind, (moment
made over) and what

use is it—you sing, and then
you hear the words, you
accompany the scene, it
goes abstract: smudge of green

for river grass, streak
of red for the river and a
greenish wash of air
for sky: blur of pretty

colors with a title: *landscape*
with house in distance.

+
And you can have the what
it all leads back to,
and you can have
this story: the man

who was a terror is the
terror in the wheelchair:
red flag on a pole
against his back means

stand to the side of the hall,
press your body
against the wall, keep
eyes on your reflection,

how it ripples on the
polished floor. Comic flag.
Coming down to, comes
down to *you can have it*—

how he wants to play chess now,
wants to remember the day,
twenty years ago, or so,
but anyway *ago,* my mother

setting up the pieces wrong
then beating him, and how
he needs to say it:
"And I never beat her again."

Then, "But that was
unfortunate wording." And
then he says it again—
"That was unfortunate wording."

What value shall we assign
his fantasy, his repetition?

+
Or maybe I came back
to discover what the river means,
how to read *that* love—
mosquitoes purring

on the dense banks, gnats
in the sticker-leaf, maggots
in the loam, and the dome
of canopy holding the world in,

holding it out (keeping it green)—
because I'm here too, in the
reflected air, with a
log, or a stone from under

for a face—and I need
the river for that reflection.

+

The story of my cowardice
goes like this: what I
tell him: tell him how
I remember that year

as the year he taught me
chess, snow coming down,
fire in the fireplace,
the year of the Christmas

he gave me the woolen jacket
with the little house
embroidered on the back,
pinks and greens so lovely

I never wore it—when there was
also the dimple in the
dining-room floor, place
where the bullet didn't

enter flesh, and cat-howls
in the distance—sucked
back from their conclusion,
which was their origin. Which

is: my sister on the porch
lumped on the ice where
he threw her in the
days before his wheelchair.

Mom at the stove, stirring
and frying, me in the rocker,
singing, while we wait for the
final explosion, the one

that will carry us finally all down
into the dark—at last.

+
Never comes. Comes
only the moment when you
have to go on, get up
look for the flashlight

in the tool drawer, the moment
when you break the scene:
you break the tune, you
risk your body because

she has a sister. That
is the only moment
left you, the moment you
can go back to. Isn't it

home now? Waiting for the
kindling point, and it's
hard to explain the marriage
of desperation and courage

but what if you had to
defend *yourself* now,
that one you gave away—
remember? There's a line

beyond which what is real
is real and if I could
live on the other side
I would know how to live.

Oil on water. Sunlight on oil.
Answer that doesn't answer.

+
Can the meaning of this river lie
in how the banks do not
define it? How it's moving
under the reflected world, swollen

as if the whole of life lay
ahead, sluggish but there, under
the sheen of a surface—ripple
in the mind's eye, moment

swept under, then
rising and spreading—thinning?

+

The story of my cowardice
goes like this: broken bottle
against your throat, *my* throat—
the *then* so that now

when he tells me to find him
something yellow I wheel the chair
over to the window, lift
the binoculars and find

the early leaf shoots
of some gnarled tree, green,
with a yellowish wash,
which I point out though

I'll never know if this
is the kind of yellow
that will do, only that a
small swift bird, true yellow,

shoots out of the lenses'
circle just as I steady it—
just as the world offers it, not
a symbol, not a promise,

just a glimmer. Or
goes like this: glimmer
that I fail
to mention. Or like this:

I bring iris. I
bring roses, scan for yellow.

+

Canopy keeping the
world green, banks gone
soggy where the river
flooded. For how long

shall I hide my face, tell me,
for it is ugly because it
knows something larger
than it fathoms, answers

to something brutal
and elsewhere that tastes
like the river and the
leaves in the gully.

Rabbit in the clearing, back
facing to me, dogs off
barking down a false
trail and I look

away and when I look back
she's still there, making
a silhouette, ears big
like in the comics, serious—

like in the comics.
And I look away because if
she's still there when I
look again, I am free

or lost, or a woman
standing by a river—
waiting and spitting to
scare her out: the *what*

it is that she means,
and meaning to last out
the dusk before looking.
What value shall we assign

the blur of her reflection?
Gardez, check, checkmate.

+
Lines of brambles webbing
my face and I
can go into the hour
of whatever I'll

give back—my thinness
and my shyness: nothing
but how I keep him, keep
you, from hurting me, body

as baggage, waiting
for music or a deeper shade
of dark to jolt it loose. Meanwhile,
Leon, and house in distance—

slime between my toes
where the river receded,
eyes averted, waiting
out the dusk, not looking—

mind patching colors
the world gives back—wanting
not to have to name it: *this*:
my banner, my white flag? You can do

anything to me, and in the end,
if I love you I will love you?

+
You start some-
where, you
start because you
have to, you

climb without
knowing you climb,
you arrive without
knowing where

you are and when
you fall there is
no difference
between the dark

and the light
and what you know.

+

So that this is not
about love anymore,
but about the body
in the song, broken

and free—a loss
like the trench of
real sky where the river
clears it: world

of blue falling
into world of black,
out in the outer
hemispheres where we

cannot see it—looking
up, sounds like weeping,
like *yes,* swells like
singing—rabbit thumping

out the beat, but who
can hear her—just the sound
of twigs snapping. Shards
of glass in bank-light,

light on a river, river
in my veins, blood in my
throat, leaves on my tongue.
About how I say it—

none of you
will ever own me, ever.

3

RATHER A PALE OCCASION FOR FLOWERS

It never was—the way you remember.
You'd zero in on fog, say, when really
what was memorable about the place
was the cacti: and you all this while
intent on how fast the wind
could carry a waft of fog on by.

Certainly, there is fire in your hair.
But when I speak of it you just say
rain, child, fireplace—*as I remember*
we cooked a lot and even now
with the stone lions waving at the end
of the driveway, with the five ginkgoes
safely installed, and neither cacti nor fog
in the forecast, there is most merely
the sensed presence of buds—
just as not long ago there was
the mere sensed presence of snow.

Even so—with or without your wanting—
the day wants on: tulips rise, crows
make a vision of the lemon tree.

—And all with a wash of nightmare
wafting through. So: you bark, you growl,
you stick out your tongue, you lie
about praying, and you are never
in any shape to drive. Nevertheless
you take the car right through the flower stand
and on into the Mississippi. No matter.
There are other issues to attend to:
how the ugly child is thought to be
more dishonest than his cute peers,
or the presidential *search we high,*
search we low—no hanky. Do they suppose
we can mop up this much blood
with our french bread? This is all
an experiment in human nonsense,—
this, our symphony of frailty.

Self-mutilation, says Dr. John Briere,
is merely the attempt not *to commit*
suicide. You warning, you cursed flower you—
walk and keep on walking. Give yourself
a dog. There is this story the body
is trying to write—and you off
creating a fate-filled portrait of the day:
(eight ball, twenty cents, goodwill): *maybe,*
yes, definitely no…ask again later.

Rather a pale occasion for flowers
I'd say, but there is no known way
to hit on the random urge that is you, *being.*

Instead, you try this, you try that,
but every year, on the Fourth of July—
try as you might to avoid it—you end up
on the LEGALIZE POT float,
waving. We shall all move back now
one square with a single cheer
for how it happens. You see it never was
the way you remember, just an idea
shaping itself into time before
departing. You even made up the lions
because their waving was sufficient
to keep you going—though barely.

So, stand to. This isn't the scene
where you flatten the rear of the squirrel,
it's the instant after, the instant before
you hit reverse and back back over the body.

POINT OF DEPARTURE

(108th at the Hudson)

Could be anything, but it's pigeons:
taking off from the sides of buildings
and heading on out like an idea
that knows where it's going—beginning,
say, with the artsy part, then moving
downward, at an angle, toward whatever
a river might be reduced to after
it's been stripped of all its meaning.

Christ, they've been loaded and unloaded
to death, but I can start with *pretty* now—
start with rivers of pigeons, a pigeon-gray
river and miles of river-gray sky—
because I know I'm going to take it back soon,
and that something in the angle we've got going here,
how we're moving through it, or maybe just
caught in it, is what's going to save us,
keep us from stalling in mid-air.

Could have been anything, but it was
pigeons came to stand for what a sense
of *beautiful,* or *order* might do to a life, i.
e.—ruin it, like thinking in place of
a bird enacting the eating of crumbs.

Not a bird, not a net: it's nothing, that thought.
So, now we've got a scene that's lost its meaning—
which is the meaning we're bent on losing.

We want the common arc a common pigeon makes
with his wing-tips when he's moving, how it's
something like a tunnel you could live in
if you could turn as he turns, not lose the path
in thinking *wing-tips like a quick note repeating*
"If you can keep me, keep me," or how *a life could*
make that kind of room by moving through it.

To follow in that tunnel, stay right behind him.
Take nothing with you. However far you get,
go farther. Rest and then go farther.

Point in the direction of Harlem,
of Soho, or of Sutton, point
in the direction of Kansas—four
ways to water, to whoever you will be
when you arrive there, which is not
whatever you think you might imagine, but more
like that idea that knows where it's going
but keeps the plan of action to itself.

This is off the beaten track of how
you must pick up your cross and keep on lurching.

Point toward Harlem, be running—
NO RADIO, NO STEREO, NO CASSETTE, NOTHING
OF VALUE but the brutal windows
of a church in sunlight, but the little islands
that are the hopeless, and how I'm not the one
to help you with that image, to burden you,
unburden you, or hope to make your mind up
concerning the issue of dust and ashes.

You can do whatever you want now.
Do whatever you want. You can
move up Broadway repeating a tune
from the airways, staying dressed, not
breaking windows—whistling and avoiding arrest.

You can walk and keep on walking.
You can walk and arrive at water.
However far you get, go farther.
You are as free as you will ever be.
You are off the beaten track
of how you might not get there,
and you can mark the distance now in inches.

WIND

shaking the night loose.

The bay tree
by the pump-house door rattles.

The bones
of the pepper tree
rattle.

Do the heifers, then,
still balance on the hillside?

Are the iris which
crowd the meadows lost then?

Buds nipped by cold?

Brambles snap in the driveway.

WHAT HAPPENS

if you can't imagine yourself
anywhere—what then?

For example: here—who is going
to polish the candlesticks? Who

is going to light the beeswax candles
when darkness begins to enter

these woods and all you can think of
is how light leaves the prairie:

darkness doesn't come in. *Prairie,*
keep me going a little longer.

LACK, THE HUMMINGBIRD

Too early, too late:
lacking in faith—
unable to function.

Skip the hummingbird—
watch the hovering.
Watch with a mighty faith.

Say the sky's malleable.
Save the bird.
Too early, too late—.

Lacking in faith?
Unable to function?
Unable to pray.

Regard the space in the sky.
Encircle the hover.
Maneuver around the malfunction?

Too early, too late—
left up to faith.
Left up to fate—.

Too early, too late?

INCOMPLETE SCENARIO INVOLVING
WHAT THE VOICE SAID

The sky that is the limit is the one
sky—*the moon: the same.* Meanwhile,
back at the literal ranch, my father

is behind the barn boiling a cougar's
head. He does this for *my* love
of skulls, my love of how the curves

and arches hold. It is his birthday.
We speak by fax. I myself have been
out back picking up the frozen bodies

of birds while the thermometer
rises—perhaps sufficiently. In my
dream all the houses burn—but the people

are rescued. In reality, if the past
were a fence it would be what
they call *goat-high and hog-tight.*

And behind us. No turning back.
The year my father left us I
was six. I washed my clothes in The Muddy

Truckee all that summer—stripped
and sank them into the deep shore, then
tugged them out of the claylike mud

and waved them around in the current.
Meanwhile, my mother was working on becoming
a resident of the great state of

Nevada. There are, after all, only
so many strategies available—meaning
who ever heard of the moon as limit?—meaning

the sky, when all is said and done,
that is the limit, is the one sky, meaning
root hog, as they say on the farm, *or die.*

THE RING AROUND THE REAPPEARING BODY

To speak of losing the F and AM waves
in the two tunnels by the Golden Gate
could be to mean if you can't bear your children's
voices, you put the children in the cellar.

But I would rather lead you to the cows
outside Stornetta's Dairy in Sonoma
who leave their calves with one heifer
and spend the day off grazing.

Still, you could get to the cows either way:
via the children and the cellar—via *that thought*—
or just by knowing how the road runs.
You could get there even with a map.

—Now, the fact is I was driving
in the other direction: my thoughts move
backward sometimes. I confess,
I am not completely in control.

But try this, if you trust me—
try to trust me—
I arrived in San Francisco early
and found a place for coffee. Simple.

The girls at the table next to mine
were faking the experiment: "Shall we write
that he moved less in the heat
even though we didn't do that part?"

Then, "Say the hairless mouse didn't get as hot,"
which struck me because I was reading
about a boy named Patrick in a Hampstead nursery—
we're in World War II now, and Patrick is singing.

Because he knows his mother
will not be coming back he's repeating
the same song over and over, and this,
I quote directly, is what he sings:

She will put on my overcoat and leggings,
she will zip up the zipper,
she will put on my pixie hat.

Some things, it seems, can't be abandoned,
because later, when they asked him
if he couldn't just shut up—only nicely—
he mimed his story in the corner.

They didn't have to look
at the zipping of the zipper, watch
the careful lowering down
of the hat, and so they didn't.

Funny, how it all veers back now
to the cellar I made up
for the sake of argument—or was it
for the sake of something truer?

Isn't this the part that matters? How it's not
just the story, or even how you read it—
kid wants his mother back, perhaps—
but how it travels, *that* it travels?

—How the story wasn't all he had: there was
also that saying it kept him with them.
Never mind how little they wanted him.
Never mind how he stood for loss.

—Never mind the dubious birth
of the hairless mouse, or the many roads
from Sonoma to the Golden Gate. Isn't desire,
for all its perversity, worth it?

I, for one, am sorry they lost him
because of how his rhythm rings—it's
the ring around the reappearing body—
and because he saved the pixie hat for last.

PROBLEM PERFORMED BY SHADOWS

Where the mind's eye comes together with the world
a woman is sleeping with her girlhood, the memory
of a dream dreamed by a stranger—by mistake

on a sunny afternoon in the back of his mind.
Mostly, he's shooting blue jays: when their shadows
meet their bodies, mind meets dream.

And the man who now cuts loose her dream
is the stranger from her woken world—
his headlights stain her bedroom wall with shadows:

deer heads on the woodpile mixing with memory,
shadows on a wall mixing in the mind,
two worlds intersecting as a single mistake.

She wants the blue jays to be killed by mistake.
She wants the shadows of deer heads to be dream.
She wants a world unstained by the mind—

but the world of shadows shadows the world
and the dream of the man is a man-made memory
and the memory is as simple as the shadow

of a man beating a woman, their single shadow
falling on the bedroom wall—a mistake.
She tells herself it is only a man as the memory

of a man, falling through the world to a wall in a dream.
The place where the shadow breaks in two is the world
she wants to get to, a place with space for the mind.

How they break, how they come together in the mind
is the problem performed by the shadows.
How it continues is the problem performed in the world.

In the house of adulthood she repeats the mistake
of jays from her girlhood who die when she dreams.
They enter their shadows with a thud—just a memory.

She thinks, *this the world, that the memory.*
She says *that the shadow, this the mind.*
The man drops his car keys on the dresser—*not a dream.*

Without headlights, the deer heads cast no shadows.
She pulls the years up around her, this mistake
is of her making—how he comes out of the world

into her dream could be a memory—a shadow
her mind let happen in the world by mistake.
She tells him she's been dreaming of the world.

4

HOUSE OF POURED-OUT WATERS

+

First there's the
one about the baby
in Boston whose mother
thought to fry him. You

may have read about it
in the papers, circa 1968—
yes, I was ten. Today,
he's a walking, talking

miracle, a monument to the
fine art of skin grafting.
The rest of us, meanwhile,
can relax—he's already

been reported, as in *to the*
Childhood Grief Center
(Minneapolis) (as in
to the Emergency

Room)...(Society for the
Prevention of Cruelty
to Children)...(Hurricane
Center) (I was joking)

(Somewhere in FL)
(a fact)—later to resurface
in the asylum, and, therefore,
to the folks in Minneapolis.

Relax. This is not his story.
I just wanted you to know.

+

Rather, what we're back to
is another take on the
saga in process—another
chapter in the story of

me and you—how what I want
is to give you something—
yes, you, via description,
and after my hot bath,

pen in hand and Mozart
on the tape machine, clean
and wanting to begin again
at yet another shoreline—

the beach as it was this morning,
dawn-fog, sun seeping through
from the unavailable background,
a world all shades of gold

and gray, their mixing
and their churning—a man
long dead providing the
score, *Exsultate, Jubilate*—

Can you hear it?
Do you want it?

+
Because there's also
how he must have
suffered to know that
kind of beauty, though

I won't say that's
what suffering is
for—still if I could
truly make a note here

I'd shape it like a
footnote on the mother,
her hunger—maybe for
a scream to match the

scream inside her, maybe
for some final silence,
outer hemispheres sucking
the sounds in, as if

to make a path from
there to here: that
arc you've got to form
in your imagination if I'm

going to have something
left to trade for what
I want to know, since what
I want to know is this:

what would you want read
to you in the moment
before your final sleep?
We will gather around you,

we will read, by the light
of candles, in hushed voices.

+

Or maybe it begins where
it always ends, maybe
it begins with the body,
my body—reappearing

like some kind of
refrain: I look down
and she's there again,
after all these years,

there because braced
in a doorframe between
a kitchen and a hall, between
children and father, paint

under her fingernails, and I
recognize her. Same globe
of too-bright light
fading the scene out, air

filling with the sounds
of human children,
weeping, then the sounds
of human anger—that

other kind of grieving—
room filling and
emptying like a great
and weary lung, heaving—

and she, in the doorway,
holding out for the space
between them, braced—
as if strung up.

I look down and
see her. I look down
and see how the rest
of her life is the rest

of my life. I ask her
to raise her eyes then, don't I.

+

I am speaking to you as a last resort.
I wanted to make a prayer.
I spent the youthful part
of a lifetime on it. It

did not read well. I moved
to be by the ocean—it's
where we came from, where we'll
go back to, after all, maybe

as ashes, maybe as flesh, maybe
as the one we didn't want to be—
the one who can be done without.
In my darker moments I

talk to the air. I pretend
you are here. This
is not presumption. Just
despair. There is blood

everywhere I go: in Safeway,
spurting across the rows
of Ajax, and the mother—blonde—
and the daughter—blonde—

wandering on by as if
nothing at all were happening.
Wherever I see them I imagine
the entrance of terror

in the specific form of a man
holding a broken bottle. It seems
I am about to witness the slaughter
but the truth is the blood

has already been spilled—
right before my mind
did the scene in. I have
some knowledge of the

basic theories of the psyche.
I have some grounding
in theories of the soul.
Everywhere I go there is blood—

no way to tell the darkness outside
from the darkness within.

+

Do you believe the colors
blind men in doorways
gesture to are real?
Sometimes I look up

and they are there, grays
and golds that are
churning—or only in that
(as in do you believe

only in that) world as a
clutter of clichés—not
just the forms in alleys
along the way, but the

way I'm trying to clear
some path right through them,
treading the thinning cusp
between knowing and

walking—understanding as the
famous booby prize, functioning
as some kind of trophy
I could perm my hair

and press a dress to collect—
then keep on washing up for—
sick with a knowledge
I can neither name

nor find the courage for, sick
with the choice I'll have
to make one fine day, sick
with fog, dawn-time, sky

shattered, sun trying, waves
trying—lovely for what
they are worth—all out beyond
the beachfront property, where

maybe it's all drifting together,
maybe all drifting apart.

+

Should have begun with the
angel in Central Park
(by Emma Stebbins, circa
1873). Do you know her?—

Feet caught in the
moment before she discovers
her weight, one hand
out for balance, wings

still full of air. Just
some metal made into
wings, just some wings
about to fold in, just

a statue, pigeons on her
head, Mozart on the
tape machine, vacuum
in the place where the

notes rise up (how he
must have suffered) life
from which something
beautiful was made, pen-in-hand

for how I want it, *Exsultate,*
Jubilate, words from elsewhere
seeping out of the unavailable
background: *though the world*

destroy this body, yet
in my flesh shall I
see God—sense of humor
standing for survival

Exsultate standing for
itself and for how
I want to hold it
out in the cup I make

of my bony hands,—
and how the cup won't hold it.

+
Dark and I come
to the note then that
almost breaks me before
it fades, clearing

the path to *elsewhere*
so I might ask you
kindly what I would
have asked in anger—

(the very least equaling
the very most here and we're
back to the angel in
Central Park and how I want

to know) if you can tell
by her face, utterly tragic,
utterly beautiful, that she
has been here before,

that *this* is the moment
of her final landing,
that she belongs to us now.
Angel at the pool of Bethez:

house of olives, house
of mercy, house of
poured-out waters,
and the story of a man

healed not with water
only, but with the water
and with the blood: rain
on metal, metal that's a

face, face that is true—
notes rising up toward
elsewhere, outer hemispheres
sucking the sound in. Then

from somewhere the coo
of pigeons. *How* elsewhere is it?

+
When I look at the photos
of Hedda, I see the one
I can't let happen. When I
look at the pictures

of Lisa I am loosed
on the world unfit, sense
of irony holding my
words together, wedge

of cruelty keeping me
human, lumbering
toward midnight-happening,
holding my fractured skull:

I may be landing,
I may be taking off—
all I want is to
give you something

before it happens, something
a person could live by.

+

Numb tongue, tongue
soaked in blood, thrumming
itself on the roof
of a mouth, sense of

humor flatter than the
Nimitz, flat place where
my life shook itself
apart, face down in the

dust, distance collapsing
under the weight of its
greatness—distance
between the life that is

yes and the life
that is *no,* ground-level
as the ever popular life
that is *maybe.* (Face down.)

Wanting something more
than how I said it—
none of you will ever
own me, ever—room of my

telling collapsing,
collapsing the space
for the place we have together.
And I wanted to give you something?

Something more than
how I said it: *Ever.*

+

I am only half-way home
but I know the things I know:
You do not destroy the ones
you hate, you only change them

into something you can do
without, something you think
you can do without. There is
a kind of freedom here,

a place I'm trying to get to—
lies with my only secret: how
when he wrenches his arm back
to slug you, what you do

is look in his eyes hard.
That look, the final betrayal—
and all you get back
is your body, blood on your

chin, tongue soaked in blood,
and a glimpse of where
you are trying to get to, place
that might finish you, place

that might save you, you
don't know—you just go
because it is where you
are going (wedge of sarcasm

keeping you sane, keeping you
distant). Distance how you
stay alive here. Boiling
down to nothing. Sometimes

it seems I am choking myself,
sometimes it seems I'm just choking.

+
Sometimes I mourn the
beach, woo the waves
out beyond the you-know-
what. At night when the

moonlight's trying to
keep us, I walk the rib
of shoreline speaking
to my soul, saying *soul,*

teach me how to dance
real slow, real quick—
just once before the moon
goes out and the lights

go down over Frisco. The
fog rolls in some more.
I hold whatever thought
I need to know it—I

hold whatever thought
might reel the soul in, I
hope they are the same
thought—I hold my

two arms out, say *soul,*
we will come to the one
o-happy end to our
defection, go endlessly

forward together—sometimes
we will call ourselves
beauty, *sometimes*
we will call ourselves

pain. *We will marry ourselves*
to the fate of the earth:
sky churning, waves
breaking, notes breaking.

Unavailable moonlight.
Acres of silence out beyond.

+
An arc that is inside
out is still an arc, the
path that leads to lightness
leads to dark: the stone

in New York that says
GOD'S ANGEL wants to mean
there was no such child
as Lisa Steinberg, means—

without wanting to—the
truth: there was only
Lisa, and she belonged
to us. I have carried

him for twenty-three years,
back curled over where he
hit the griddle, and I
hand him back now, and I

take him with me—silence
at the end of the tape receding.

5

NOTES TOWARD A DEFINITION

*

Maybe we start with the part about how
we embody the theory of dust
and ashes now, that pure place beyond
image and story and voice—*those* lies.

Maybe we start with the dark room,
you in it, skeletal, waiting, for the pieces—
not to come together even, but just to
surface—let us begin with Baudelaire:
Sorrow be wise, be calm and how
any old-time biker, any Person-In-Black,
any girl from the suburbs
with her head shaved bald could tell you—
there's no music in the background
that can help you.

For now I shall sleep in the dust
and thou shalt seek me in the morning
but I shall not be. That's Job.
And *this* is where you begin,
begin by blowing smoke on a bug
to move him without moving your knee,
and this part wants to leave a space
to overlap the moment when you'll notice—
now that you've numbed him in his tracks—
the white stripe on his wings, gold stripe
like eyeliner at its rim, and think
like eyeliner, but perfect. And all this
by the light of a cigarette.

*

What I meant to say about chaos theory
is that the important part is *not* the theory,
not even the chaos, but the mind, how it
lays itself down over century after century—
(*like eyeliner*, like *like)* and then
the obliging centuries—like a thought
saying *maybe it's the overlap of mind*
upon the centuries, the shape of which
is perfect—that part rising now, beyond your reach
regardless of how much you want it.
Then, *maybe it's a shadow.*

Shall we cross the river now
and rest in the shade of the trees?

Stonewall, dying, speaks thusly to his troops,
but the troops have vanished, they are
boycotting the river, they are
boycotting the shade of the trees,
they have boycotted the dying man's dream—
they are in a dark room waiting for the pieces
to surface. They are listening for silence,
but what they hear is the blood
making its way by their ears.

*

When I say my bed shall comfort me,
my couch shall ease my complaint,
then thou scarest me with dreams
and terrifiest me through visions.

Then Descartes, groping back toward God
in the God-filled room: *I think, hence* et-
cetera. But they called reason
good sense back then, and who can blame them,
God arriving at the doorstep just in time—
holding the puzzle's only missing piece.

Author of the voices in their heads.

I think, hence hence—hence
(…three centuries, four decades, nine years,
God only knows how many days, and counting…)
your voices are not your own,
you are nothing. Then *All poetry*
is a form of prayer—but that's Keats,
voice of a sacred century.

I do not think they understood that what
they were asking for, in the end, was
the image and the story of our bodies.
I do not think they believed
in how thoroughly we could love them.

*

That music in the background, trying to be
of use: it seems so strange to hear you say
in the course of a lifetime, over and over—
I've never been laid so low.
And that's the sound of the river
of blood in your head, laughing, saying
just put it back somehow together.

Century as the voices in our heads.
Mousetrap in the corner snapping NOW
in the backward-moving mind.
Imagine yesterday. Imagine
the sound of a horse eating acorns.

And what if the wind really is
moaning as it makes its way past our ears?
Can you live behind this soul?
Never stopping to think it.

That music in the background, trying again
to be of use—it's in the background, it's
trying to be of use. Well, here's to it,
and to the back turned toward the river—
the ending, some ending, somebody's ending.
We couldn't resist, we put this room in.
Here's to how we *had* to do it.

*
It is fall. Yesterday was Thursday.
You were right—remember, you said it
yourself, there's an edge beyond the edge
and it belongs to us. I would do anything
to pull you through. Anything
to pull through. Tule fog rising,
curling in the edges of the paper,
writing it down now—how you will rise
and go calmly to the kitchen, take down
the bowl. Looking for cereal. Looking for milk.

Listen.—I present these things in order
of appearance, not because that is the order
in which you must now make them happen
but because, as it happens—they can also
be arranged this way in order
to present a progression.

HOWEVER,

what if I said I wanted
myself back whole—what then?

"What's broken, we can fix,"
the humans would say—predictably.

You have to love them for that.

Of course, nothing *really* heals.

I know what the wind knows.
Tearing across the prairie,

bits of grit riding its cold storm—
grit like coal dust, or like ashes:

What's the difference?
There's enough love here.

THE SEVENTH REVELATION OF MY THIRTY-SEVENTH YEAR

You can take it as a matter
of course: this matter of how
anything your attention falls on

means: *there's this again, that*
yours should be a rocky life—
nothing but scrapes and sighs

to steer by—: so that even if
you *were* the sort of person
to be stopped in your tracks

by tomatoes in a shop window—
vines still attached, vines
like wax, the flawless fruit

like a model for fruit—even if
you were, you'd take it
as a prophecy for your coming

arrest, get drunk, fall asleep
on the CamBus and get arrested—
returning, upon your release,

through the unoccupied swirling
of the snow to your small
brown house on the floodplain—

or you could take this life,
so badly broken in, and say
instead, say, *I lay me down now*

like a lace of ripples
in sand, by the wild
and lovely Atlantic.

LACK, THE WILLOW

The good earth spins and circles.
  The *willow* speaks from the center.

The willow speaks with a record force.
  The warning is retrospective.

The universe raises the body.
  We respond with our lives.

We respond with our lives?
  Yes—I carry this feather wherever I go.

I thought that was interpretation.
  It is our lives.

Our minds make a wedge.
  The language is breaking.

You call the feather something else?
  Later, it will be my home.

Where the leaf trembles and the ant marches?
  Where my ghost will come home to rest.

Horses need a place to come home to, to drown.
  I carry this feather wherever I go.

The mind's a mysterious master.
    The world is a wedge.

Aren't we born with a light in our eyes?
    The mathematics of stars and planets.

Aren't we born with a storm in our brows?
    The willow is the record force.

The flat hands of moles pat the ground.
    Tunnel of fear, tunnel of grief.

Nothing can protect them?
    We have lost that argument.

Truth or innuendo?
    I carry this feather wherever I go.

The warning was retrospective.
    I carry the warning, I carry the feather.

Fear is a place to come home to, to drown?
    I carry this feather.

Respond with your grief.
    I respond with this feather.

The good earth spins in darkness?
    I carry this feather.

    I carry this feather wherever I go.

I HAVE BEEN LIVING

I have been living
closer to the ocean than I thought—
in a rocky cove thick with seaweed.

It pulls me down when I go wading.
Sometimes, to get back to land
takes everything that I have in me.

Sometimes, to get back to land
is the worst thing a person can do.
Meanwhile, we are dreaming:

The body is innocent.
She has never hurt me.
What we love flutters in us.

THE PRAIRIE AS VALID PROVIDER

1.

Occasionally, I start from scratch.

Scratch for me is the prairie
and moonlight is my favorite season—
white when it lies,
white when the rain pours over,
white when it doesn't.

I can hear the sheep crying
in the driving rain—lightning
catches the world as an image
might catch history.

Then the prairie goes on
a long way, and it looks
like the sheep are just grazing.

Rot enters the rolled hay.

2.

Stepping right over what I started to say—
there's the *ha ha* of it.
Not this pit of my personal making
but *our* pit.

Not how when the city I love
shook itself down,
the bodies in the highway sandwich
smelled for days—
but how the kids in the mosh pit
kept on dancing.

Theirs is an informed despair—
it's all sweat and bashing,

but when they rise up,
thin shadows in the bluish light,
and plunge back toward the field
of up-stretched arms—they know
those arms will catch them.

They know the crowd will hold them up
as long as it can.

Speaking strictly for myself here,
I'd say that that's a lot to know.

3.

It's true.
This is about love.

Could have been love
for the cryptic mysticness of happiness
as a thought.

But there was a man I loved
in that city.

Don't know how I ended up
back at scratch—on a green planet
watching the lightning,
mind like a minor civil division,
metabolism adrift and some
crucial parts missing.

The crocodile skull on the windowsill
is watching the prairie
for signs of change.

I am watching the croc
for signs of a name.

For a long time now
I have known
I was going someplace impossible—

I have known.

Olive, willow, memory.—

This is for the hypnotic jasmine
that grows outside my window.

4.

Exactly what kind of sleep
do you think you could use?

Like a flash for the world
to take shape in.

(This
is no place for contradictions.
No place for argument.)

I run water in the tub.
I turn off the lights
and light the floating candles.

When they sail under the leaky faucet
there's a hissing that could be
flesh burning, but isn't.

In the dark the voice continues—
Lie still my dear, sleep sweet.
(Might be something I read,
but it sounds like my guardian angel.)

Is everything all right?

No, but lie still all the same.

5.

I miss him
like the end of the world
at the end of the century.
In which nobody wrote *Fidelio*.

Enough to make you want
to explode a sentence?

Enough to make me.

But the sentences have all been exploded.
I checked.

Book, bookmark, bed—we shall now
empty one out: one sentence:

"I heard a child asking
Where its legs were"
(By Grand Central Station
I Sat Down and Wept)

—and somewhere on a dark platform
a door opens on a history
and quickly slams shut.

And quickly slams shut?
And quickly slams shut.

As with "somewhere else
there was a bombing."

And somewhere else.
I can't tell you
the who and whom of it.
Can't even tell you the price
of the morning paper.

Just help me pull the bodies
out of the mud.

Grab that arm and drag. Good.

Now work a little faster.
This is not just any field.
This is a field of art.

6.

The moon and the sheep and the hay and the rain.

Once upon a time
there was a *once upon a time.*

Because I loved,
because I failed
came the space for greater sorrow.

What, if anything,
do we know?

How to make a bomb?
How to unmake a sentence?
How to rate a sorrow
on a scale from one to ten?

What the prairie said
was mercy the sky
refuses. Truth hovers
over the feasible landscape:

There is no god.
Loneliness is the lesser pain.

If I can be of use—call me.

7.

This is for the kids in the mosh pit.
Lie still my dears, sleep sweet.
The sentence the angels unraveled
the wind plays back as music.

Angels? What angels?

Play that back as music.

The music in the mosh pit's
hard enough to make you think of hate.

And when you listen to the words?

When lightning flashes on the prairie
it's gold all over green—all over.

And when you listen to the words?

O.K.—when you listen to the words
you know that they want life
just like we did, only harder.

Play that back as music.

Really the grass has tufts of white?

And the jasmine has yellow flowers.

THE USABLE FIELD

For Giles Mead

(1928-2003)

In memoriam

THE DEAD, LEANING (IN THE GRASSES AND BEYOND THE TRENCHES,—LIKE OAKS)

In the high and mighty grasses
the dead lean on the living
like nobody's business,—

they think we are their mission.
Thus the rain, whereby they say
now wash your eyes and pray.

Pray for anything but forgiveness.

In the trenched terrain the shadows
in people identify with mountains—
the people have to be rodents

if they want to debate. Else,
there's just the undignified
nature of revenge, inheritance

and innuendo, being and dint—
not even a breeze to soften
the ought. For this is the tumor

of living among them—
if there is death between you
and the oak, there is no oak.

I

TO WHATEVER REMAINS

This is some chant I'm working at—
tired on tarmac and disaster,
best I can do these days is hope

for some way to keep the rote days rote.
Hard to tell what's safe,
hard to tell what's wise. Fog means:

unlock the geese from the sky—at your
own risk, at your peril.
But the truth is I pass that harp

to the disappeared soul, saying soul
sing me something, speak of the
best dream—that's a beginning.

Tired on tarmac, this keeps me going—
but barely. Where's the disaster
that would be enough? What's that beauty

in the last light leaving for the day?
Anything to do with how I-880 tops the hill
and heads on down toward San Jose?

Soul, sing me something of how the good earth
heals. Sing me something soon. As if
being asked to celebrate created things.—

As if being passed the harp and asked to sing.
Do it before the crow at the dog bowl exits.
Do it before life goes taut as a new scar.

Before the fog lifts, before the geese
fly over in Air Force formation.

SOME DAYS

I hide in the river
with a reed to breathe through.
The river carries me

slowly downstream.
Luna calls it the bit
where I converse with slime.

She says it's just a part
of a larger step, she says
she can't believe I don't

know how the dance goes.

AND THEN THE SMOKE—

sole residue of written wisdom
as actualized by things.
Christ if the tulips shudder.

Here the grass is rain-flattened
and may not re-spring. What
can one person say to another?

The master is the master?
The children are playing on the shore?
To this language, the heron on the sandbar

does not answer.
Objects sought after.
Objects retrieved.

The season of rain passes.
The master is not the master.

THREE CANDLES
AND A BOWERBIRD

I do not know why
the three candles must sit
before this oval mirror,

but they must.——
I do not know much
about beauty, though

its consequences
are clearly great—even
to the animals:

to the bowerbird
who steals what is blue,
decorates, paints

his house; to the peacock
who loves the otherwise
useless tail of the peacock—

the tail *we* love.
The feathers *we* steal.
Perhaps even to the sunflowers

turning in their Fibonacci
spirals the consequences
are great, or to the mathematical

dunes with ripples
in the equation of all things
windswept. Perhaps

mostly, then, to the wind.
Perhaps mostly to the bowerbird.
I cannot say.

But I light the candles: there is
joy in it. And in the mirror
also, there is joy.

THE RIVER ITSELF

Gretel chomps the shadow
of a crow, and the crow
falls—as the crow flies,

so to speak—into
the smashed corn.
Some of this happens

in a field, some
in the quarter-pounder
that is Gretel's brain.

Also there is a bus
caught on a bend in the river.
The bus needs work.

Let me introduce myself:
I am Luna, keeper of the dachshund,
the dachshund Gretel

to be precise. One of the sorriest
shapes man ever thought up
when it comes to stomping

the muddy fields.
But talk about swimming—
Gretel swims like an angel.

Gretel is,
to be precise,
a short-leggèd angel.

I myself am Luna.
Wind.
There's a storm

named after me—just look
what it has done
to the banks of this river—.

Regard the ill-fated bus
and ask me if I give a damn.
Say *Luna, do you give a damn?*

I say crow.
I say wind.
It's a river.

I say look at the light
playing on the earth—
and take it, so to speak,

with a grain of salt.
Or take it elsewhere—
Gretel would.

WE TAKE THE CIRCUS
TO ANOTHER LEVEL—

we, who are not afraid to die,—we remember how
to love nothing. No blue jay in the pepper tree, no
crocus blooming on the compost, and most steadfastly

no rye-grass-swaying-in-breezes. No breezes.
No fetish of turtle carved from jade. The palmist
says *trees together, trees apart: the odds*

by definition can't conspire. Still, we are
the future in which the ankle breaks. We keep
records of what is harvested and what is due

and the records own us, who never think of elsewhere
as a mission. In our unhurried gloom, we are just
a grave away from the truth: the mechanism

of grief supplies no answer. *Hearts empty*
says the palmist, *hearts with blood in them.*
The act of grieving is not required.

The odds, by definition, can't conspire.

YOU ARE NOT REMOVED

until the light
    washes over you—

and the light has *not*
    washed over you.

You need to love the gnats
    swirling over the toxic

swamp (for the swamp is *always*
    toxic) you need to

catalogue mazes and map
    adamancies, get

chokecherries to grow
    next to sage—

unleash even
    the slightest allegiance

and *then* let the light
    wash over you.

THE PART — AND THE WHOLE OF IT

Stocking the globe is not
my issue, taking stock
is my issue—and deciding

what to do next. I was
only a speck until the machine
got a hold of me. I'd curl up

and read my accounts. It was
another world—built on dead trees—
on the shores of mirror and veil.

Now—men and women speaking:
Same audit, same flinch.
Same tongue—no visible shore.

Home is another story:
different specks, same machine.
Prescription or sacrifice—

it's hard to say, but always
the same relentless fever—
on the tattered wing of day.

WOODS HOLE

Window to the sea. Bells
are ringing. The road
to the south is blue—

all over the dunes
rose-hips bloom. All
over town—bells. Many

are the ways, but there
is only one road
home, and it is not

for you. All over
town—and the road
to the south is blue.

GIFT HORIZON

Turn the head of the bird he says
and dies, leaving us in the rain
and his painting unfinished. Turn

the head of the bird. We haven't
got a clue (and it raining)—so, slowly,
we learn to love moss and even the sheen

of green algae inside the water trough. Not
a clue and it always (the trough)
suggesting a future of gray horses—

the trail muddy, the child bruised
long before the shadowy race begins.
Nor is the woman singing, she's crying.

He painted her as if singing because
he was broken and would have stolen
anything to heal himself.

POINT AND COUNTERPOINT
IN ALL THINGS

It is easy for the mind
to hold *magnolia* in its wings
at a time when the magnolia

is blossoming,—scattering its famous
petals, (famous white, rimmed
with famous brown) around your doorstep—.

It is easy to understand the importance
of linen or to give of yourself
until there is no self. But when the book

is opened to the page about magnolias
then where will you be? There is
a talisman called *mercy*, there is

a single blossom—called *commence*.

SISTER HARVEST
BROTHER BLUES

Because there is no earth-light,
because there is none other, we remain
wayward and hampered. No one

will be going this day with us.
The main force is the usable field
or sun on the useless bunchgrass,—

alchemy that spells and spells us
just as the weather spells us
and the good earth *field.* Rain

by morning and the earthworms
surface. Meanwhile, gathering
facts enough for continued serving:

mosquito-fish for the horse trough,
dented washtub by the spring
where the deer drink, drowned rat

bald and bloated in the barrel
by the stream. What is the science *for*
that leads us doe-eyed into the source

of our unmaking? Or, at the source
there is an answer—? Manufactured
instincts, and on the lawn now roughly

thirty-seven strong and busy starlings.

ALL WADING HAS WINGS

A picnic by the river
would be the right
thing, despite the secret

holding water, secret
holding of water—then
not, and the day

holding its hours
then not, then the moon
through which you see

the fish and rocks—
forgetting sometimes
even about the water.

BY REASON OF LIGHT—

There have been many—
Who called in the ships.—
Ships in off the dark water.

Instinct one minute—
Satire the next.—
There have been many.

From one vision to the next—
It is a long distance.
You have to carry a moth through rain.

You have to sleep under an upturned boat.
You have to actually *be* there.
As in *willing to die for same.*

And you have to be willing to live.
As in *I will trade you tomorrows—.*
As in no known shore, no meaning.

IF THE FIELD IS REAL

Early in this summer
of the old trees blowing down
I plant flowers—send

the dead away, one by one,
and plant flowers. We are,
now, township by township—

rough at the edges, trees
snapped, brush burning.
I plant flowers—send

the dead away, one by one.
Half my oak down, half
trying to live, mulberry

rough at the edges, trees
snapped, brush burning—
a statue of splinters.

I mow the field—
half my oak down, half
trying to live, mulberry

where the chipmunk hid. I burn
what is left of my trees—
a statue of splinters.

I mow the field
in what is left of the field—
goldenrod at the fence-line

where the rabbit hid, I burn
what is left. My trees
turn to soot. Soot

of goldenrod at the fence-line.
Hollyhocks in what is left
of the field—soot on pink,

soot on red, on white.
Hollyhock. Hollyhock.
The rasp of my voice—

a small sooty sound.
I plant flowers. We are
now, township by township

rough at the edges, trees
snapped, brush burning—
early in this summer

of the old trees blowing down.

II

MYTH

The woman in the ordinary
cloth—came here with a vision:
point and counterpoint

in all things. Stitch by stitch
she wove our world—print
of pear tree, color of moss

delighted. Colors of silk.
Outside, the crack in the pathway
opened, rain spilled in—*tomorrow*

said the rivulets, *sorrow*
to the seas. Homeless, homeless—
heaved the low sky. Mist

entered the garden. Twilight
entered the mist. Lemon-cut
of the geranium lifted too.

She did not want the scent, she
wanted the blossom. But the blossom
faded in the fading light

and the clear voice of leaves
then said *it is all just wrestling*
and turning—*before the windows*

of the dead: And the geranium,
and the mist, and the pear tree—
all shifted slightly in a single wind.

BEFORE THE FIRST ERRAND

(—which was her life on earth)
there were the practice moments:
the stars from no perspective,

the stockyards in winter. Thud
of mallet on skull—from no
perspective. In this way

she came to sense a manner of
being she wasn't there for:
the wide burst of pigeons

at dawn was not enough to keep her
from being carried in whatever
direction the changing wind suggested.

But eventually—she sensed her boy
had passed under the leviathan's
jawbone into the graveyard overlooking

the sea. She knew there was no way
to reach him, knew he would
lie on his mother's grave forever—

stunned beyond all reason, unconsoled,
that gray-as-the-answer would enter.

And the hills are messy with golden stalks.
The gray of the ocean is with him always.
The reddish fall vines, and the grave of the sky.

SHADOW DAY

She never even asked him
not to paint them, she
knows *no-point-in-asking*

when she meets it—she
only asked that he count
the bodies, particularly

the children, bodies
or heads—but history
is myth in the making,

history is water
he told her. She wanted
hard facts, he gave her

the world in motion.

THE COMPLEXITY OF MUSIC

At the bottom of music
a phrase is missing:
The white mist is coming

or *We shall be as if deserted*—.
Ocean all around us,
ocean and white mist—

(a cavern of darkness
where the phrase is missing
at the bottom of music)

where a phrase is missing.
From the floor of the ocean
a song goes out as vibration—

the water resists.
At this depth the song
has no chance. The woman

who waits for the song
will disappear into waiting.
At this depth the song

has no chance—save
she is at the bottom
of a phrase in the ocean

and the music around her—
is known as dark water.

WAS LIGHT

at the bottom
there, tomorrow,——

else where I
missed it? *And*

where I missed it?

LUNA IN THE HOUSE
OF ALL MY LONGING

Scrub this world clean.
Begin with a dream.
Do you even dream.

Enter the house
of magnolia. Enter
the magnolia tree.

See? So she
puts her arms up,
wiggles her fingers,

moths and butterflies
butterflies and moths.
She performs a plea.

With Fruit Loop dust
all over her face—
who can resist her?

We enter the house of magnolia.
We enter the blossom.
We enter the tree.

HINT

And what about
the life of the body?
Is there *there* a single grief

you will believe in?
There are geraniums
on the doorstep, bug-eaten

at the blossom and at
the leaf: you can pinch off
the dead parts, you can

water, you can turn away—
but you cannot stop yourself.

THE HABIT OF RESISTANCE

That toxic drive—
a pure urge
of sorts: numbers

as numbers, function
in progress. Each fall
a new beginning.

The wings in the trees
are black. The buildings
crumble, the asphalt

cracks. Every spring
we count the dead:
The unlucky. Sometimes

we call them the lucky.
The years: a melody
of the lucky: a curtain

of lace, a wing
of sorts. Make no mistake—
each time we cry. What

do the weeds know, where
is the justification
for the weeks, the endlessness

of days, the incorruptible
urge: Function in progress?
Numbers as numbers?

The wings in the trees
are black, the fear
in the wings comes back—

endlessness of days
and then the end.
We itemize our

tenderness, we itemize
our dead. Make
no mistake—each time

we cry. We carry
our grief whole, we
carry our lives. Swayed

by the under-self,
it's how we love.

PRINCE OF FIRE
PRINCE

Though the almanac hang
between us, though my brow
and my hands are maps—

I will encircle you
as I encircle you now
when my brow and my hands

are ash. We will be
as if chosen. Even the air
will have to pretend.

ON THE SHORES OF RIVERS AND SEAS
WE ADMIRE OUR THINKING

We make rules and think by them—
and call it *good* thinking: Foundation.
Structure: We think the river

runs *by* not *through*: the current—
dispensable, the shore—coincidence,
the sky—a margin, a margin

with far limits, but a margin.
Our symposium on the question
assumes the viewer—some seas being

too salty to believe in. We *do*
ask many questions. Whoever
wants to answer, answers: this is not

based on seaweed and trees. It is
based on knowledge—which is based
on seaweed and trees. There is

also falseness: the true sky,
for example, doesn't always
figure in,—some seas being too salty.

THE HIGH HITHER, THE EMBRACE

The stairs to the marketplace where we were
all going to speak the same language—were littered
with the elaborate cruelties of history,

the injustice of water, the shed and chasm
side by side. The stairs to the experiment
in which I meant to convince you we spoke

the same language—were our unleashing:
a dream in prose in which I'm trying
to miss you. But history will have none of this,

as far back as I can hear it: The mudflats
usher in tadpoles and onion grass: the sweet,
sweet earth, aroused.—The Empire ushers in flesh:

The high hither: the you: the embrace.

IT WAS NOT ANYTHING AFTER ALL?

Thus the wind and the dark
sage sea. Thus the wingèd wave
means *you can't have it.* And the dark

stars and the light stars too—
irreversible heavens, earthly butcher,
invisible shadow, bilge-pump,—you.

The butcher says later
is soon enough. He looks for a stone
to sharpen his blade. All manner

of knowing pushes up, out of
visibly nowhere,—and essential:
mindlessness and seagulls, trembling

and clean: we wore our Easter bonnets
and prayed. Mother booked a ticket
to the islands—extravagant picnic

by the dark sage sea. Mother says later
is soon enough, all manner of knowing
pushes up, out of visibly nowhere—and clean.

THE WORLD HOLDING OUT

It was given us
to see and, seeing, know

wholeness in the dog
in chase, familiarity

in the rabbit's cry,—
signature of blood on snow.

THAT WHICH CAME OF NOTHING
COMING ALWAYS

I have been hearing
the wind in this stand
of white pines ever

since I heard it
for the first time.
I have been hearing

the small fast river—
bright din beneath which
the waters splinter

off smooth rocks. I
have been hearing
this icy symphony

ever since I heard it
for the first time.
We are two women, walking

toward an unclaimed
expanse of horizon,
the fray of history

all around us—
and we carry everything:
the fragmentation of water,

stalactite I buried
with Willa, here
on Tina's farm where

we're half hidden
in the white pines, half
loving the icy wind.

THE WOMAN WHOSE
SPECIALTY IS LIGHT—

weathers a marsh of darkness:
night like a smudge, the day-moon
disappearing with the day,

the night-moon never coming.
Fog in the cattails is born here.
Details from an origin for the woman

whose specialty is light—light
as a book left open, the page
random, the thought she

returns to—looking for choice.
And if she gives this bruise-light
back, if she neglects the working

night, neglects the cattails,
swamp or fog—she will lose them
for now and for always, back into

the house of maps. Light
in halos, light plowing off
the dawn, pawing at the edges

of this very day—dispersing.

SEVENTY FEET FROM
THE MAGNOLIA BLOSSOM

there is an ant.

He is carrying
a heavy load.—

We should help him.

GYPSUM WHEN YOU ARRIVE

For just as there is alabaster
in the marketplace there is
the remembrance of gypsum

in the sun,—when the body
watches. If you listen
you will turn toward a remote

and ancient calling: *alien:*
you survive: beyond the brownish air
around the globe, another

streaked sky waits—as if for
a *flickering-of-wings* which it cannot
contain. As if for the flinch

in your voice.—Which it can.

THE CRYPT OF THE HOUSE

that she was born in echoes
larger than the house itself
ever was. As a girl, summers

every morning for years,
she carried the small dog
down to the river and sang

and sang to her. This much
is still available: it is
no wonder that the light

was laced—there were trees
everywhere along the banks.
No wonder that she didn't

have a name for what
compelled her: in fall
the patterns of geese

told a story about patterns
of geese in spring. The girl
charmed the world, she made

what she saw into something
to see her. The woman
lies in wait on the banks—

endless study in fracture
and repair, crypt of nooks
crypt of crannies. The light

is green, but the map
of that county is torn along
the line where the river ran.

THE ORIGIN

of what happened is not in language—
of this much I am certain.
Six degrees south, six east—

and you have it: the bird
with the blue feathers, the brown bird—
same white breasts, same scaly

ankles. The waves between us—
house light and transform motion
into the harboring of sounds in language.—

Where there is newsprint
the fact of desire is turned from again—
and again. Just the sense

that what remains might well be held up—
later, as an ending.
Twice I have walked through this life—

once for nothing, once
for facts: fairy-shrimp in the vernal pool—
glassy-winged sharpshooter

on the failing vines. Count me—
among the animals, their small
committed calls.—

Count me among
the living. My greatest desire—
to exist in a physical world.

WAS LIGHT,—

was next week with a garden
in it, next winter with the glow
of the unborn. My back

up against the mountain, face
to the snowy field,—glassy
branches of the apple tree.

If there was a mistake somewhere
I didn't know it, I only knew
the deodar choked on sky,—despite

the rumor of unaltered roots.
The essential and noble
insects burrowed. Blades

of grass mixed with snow.
I only know there is limited
liability for each party—:

the integrated lives of ants
and geese, the upturned
feet of dead rodents: corrupt

parade—as in this labor
leads to blood in the heart.
Water running over the grave.

The light drives forth
inside the head. Inside
and outside. Two beams

which must now intersect.

THE KNOWING-SHORE

The calamity at Babel
aside, the science
of the greater

and of the lesser
lights aside, and all
the abundance and terror

of commerce between
men of the products
of nature and art

aside, there are still
to consider the cones
of the deodar, turning

as they do turn,—
purple in the fall
in the southeastern

United States, but not
on the Left Coast
where they stay green

longer, through
winter even, so that
we could, then, still,

couldn't we, take it
for a sacred
mission after all,

the garden, its terse
violet, violent
rose, Rose of Sharon—

or is it only that
in a form of knowing
since abandoned,

the wish went out
and the thought
received, habit

of world made
habit of mind—
but that now: violet,

rose, purple
cones, *desolate*
theme park,—desire

aside now, life
of my life, heart
of my heart,—abandoned?

TO THE WREN, NO DIFFERENCE
NO DIFFERENCE TO THE JAY

I came a long
way to believe
in the blue jay

and I did not cheat
anyone. I
came a long way—

through complexities
of bird-sound and calendar
to believe in nothing

before I believed
in the jay.

III

THE LADEN HENCEFORTH PENDING

My assignment was *one useful plan,*
to make one useful plan of the surrounding
thirteen hundred acres of chaparral

and oak, manzanita and bunchgrass
in the season of the oak's unfurling,
in the season of the blue-eyed grasses,

wind-washed and rain-swept and moving
toward the scorch of summer,——*make*
an afternoon of it, he said.

Three dogs came with me up the hill
named for its sugar-pines, to what
we call the *little pike*——that farthest

meadow of my childhood,——the red head
of the vulture bent with watching,
the red tail of the hawk spread wide.

Your memory casts a shadow when you
go into the future, and the shadow
wants to know what owns you——the red

and lichened trunk of the madrona
or the twin dry creeks converging as matter
and lack of matter meeting. You have to be

nothing, take whatever amnesty is offered—
the case for love is not the case
for tragedy revisited, or there is

for certain now—a laden henceforth pending.

TRANS-GENERATIONAL HAUNTING

They come to you in dreams,
the dearly departed. They
come to you again and again—
elsewhere and otherwise included.

The same.

Then facing the purple mountain
and her shadow, I am watching
to keep them from slipping away.

I look inward—
I look outward—
All the same.

I was loved.
I was loved
and I return—

everywhere the dead
calling my name.

THE FLESH IS FEAR

and the compass—unfettered
by true north. The sky
hangs open—to breathe

is to shift just a little
toward earth, necessary
earth,—recounting for all

it is worth the problematic
acting-out of air, the flaw
in the green of the forest.

Not careful, not loyal.
Keep going the wind.
An event worth noting.

The singer of virtues
travels the short line back
from diamonds to coal—.

Keep silence, she says,
keep luck—some great thing
is crossing our path, into dusk.

LIMINAL

Where the yellow thistle
comes into its own,
home to bunchgrass,

oak, madrone, where
the hunters set out
for the bridge across

eternity, *buckeye*
antler, bone,—your
deer-colored dog

is loping in the
deer-colored grass
in the morning. *Nowhere*

are you where we are not.

SAME AUDIT, SAME SACRIFICE

I spent half my life talking to you
and I never got an answer. That's a kind
of sailing you wouldn't call sailing

unless you had to. I wanted to know
about the earth and the sea—about
the unleashed moments. I marked the days,

I measured the snowfall, in summer
I washed my feet in buckets. In fall
while other people were sporting

bright sweaters and carrying home
bags of tomatoes, I watched
the shadow of the barges, watched

the dragging of the river,
the moment and the specter—then
I took the selfsame audit.

HEART
(SNOW FALLING)

Heart, no matter what door you return through—
inches falling,—in pitch of night confettied,
in dawn-light: no matter: I will put you out

over and again until what matters most—
the not knowing of what I do not know—
rises in the now moonlight as the final inch

begins to crust toward shine and I speak so:
Go out, heart, into it. Do not return. Because mine
is a body caught, because submit is not your answer—

and because you, like the enchanted moon, are good.

HIGH CLIFF COMING

Fate's a stable lesson
after all: the trees
can't grow into the

prevailing wind—the
bird-like hands
can't fly.

Where the waves fold back
and the high cliff guides—
this elegy

keeps the heart
beating and the blood
from going cold

while the nerves
web the body—
the body-dream.

SOMETIMES THE MIND

is taken by surprise
as it speaks: *are you
sure this is the right street?*

for example—or just
cow-path—no more: a blurb,
a bleep, really, out of

the imagination, and then
once again everything is
perfectly still, save, perhaps,

a cow or two on the horizon,—
and the sound of cowbirds
in sudden excellence, where

formerly there were none.

WITH NO PRAISE
FROM THE FAR DARK REACHES

I believe in the horse and the marshes—I believe
in the crow,—talisman of apple tree and pear.
I believe in the wall. This wall and the other.

Did I say the willow? I believe the willow
knows what the dead know, passing over.

Unmeasurable dust from here to the nearest star—

keep circling, for if I believe in our mutual
intervals of response and longing, all the more
do I believe in how the animals take themselves

somewhat sadly off into the shrubbery and damp grasses
toward the roughly longed-for passage. The Tradition.

The grasses. I believe in the dust and the grasses.

SPECULATION

I do not think that love will reach the dead—
and, the seven weeks of sorrow pending,
I do not think they should have much regret:
the marginalia and mania survive them
and that was all they might have taken.

My own destiny is hard enough to salvage
from the safety pins, the thin discs of soap—
the plenty and the lack converging, the left hand
of the dead laid over the right hand
of the living, the left hand of the living
laid over the right hand of the dead.

I do not think the shadow of the cloud
is sign, until the hawk lays *his* shadow down.
I have no proof the dead survive the call.

IN GRIEF
THE PILOT KNOWS YOU

In grief, the pilot knows you—
no need to say *take me to my so-called soul*—
she *is* your so-called soul: she knows
you will be waiting when she lands—she wants
you to be with her if you drown.

In the spring, we lost our innocence

and took center stage. Fall
was the time of harvest, just as in summer
there was bounty in the wind-sound
and the farmer-self learning her lessons

from the vines and then the rows of vines—
bounty in the one voice joined
to the multitude of its own becoming.

In winter, the grit on the wind is the single
candor we live by—and while the far shore
and the cliffs beyond it are fogged in—

it does not occur to us to weep:
a shore is not a shore without her.

LABYRINTH

Tomorrow,—by reason of rapture.
Rapture—by reason of pain.
There is tomorrow in it

and we look away.
There is tomorrow in the one
God-given stone, and we look away.

When we look away we look into
the past. We get down on our knees
in sorrow. We are much too stunned

to pray. The truth about today
was a bright stone shining—.
By reason of nightmare, by reason

of pain, by reason of wit revisited.
By reason of madness, whosoever
begins shall be asked to finish.

THE WOMAN IN THE ORDINARY CLOTH

came here with a mission.
Work by work there starts a world
that the vines and poppies finish.

At night the coyote songs
stir a vision: the vineyard
and the grave are one. By day

the dead inhabit the canyons,
the living weed the vine-rows
and she wanders between them—

calls the months *bunchgrass, thistle*
coyote-brush. Afternoons on the hillside
two large madrones create the circle

of shade in which she is now sleeping.

THE SPECTER AND HIS WORLD
ARE ONE

Some say a jar can tell you
where you are, some say
a satellite. Others—

the postman, the stars,
the sea. It is possible
for the world to mislead you.

You cannot look too much
over your shoulder.
The symbol for moss

is a symbol for destiny:
The shut blaze darkens.
The world misleads you.

You cannot look too much
over your shoulder, I
cannot but say now

follow me,—onto the road
my own heart made,—
the red disc—

the real clay—
pile of yellow thistle
where I'm weeding.

This is the red earth *you* loved
—my way into.

                    (*for my father, in memoriam*)

WHERE IN THE STORY THE HORSE MAZY DIES

&
Anymore the rain that matters, anymore the thistle.
And never matter the *word* as a way of being for:
In the era of *postmodern* and *maybe*

the mammals still strike up friendships.
I let the vines cover these windows on purpose.
Neither laziness nor doubt—but memory.

I was the wind, and the needle she went for.
I was the bridge and halt to elsewhere—
and the book that told the lie survives.

Eagle topping the deodar, barn owls in the palms,
moss on the roof where the old shed sags.
The magpie will be here for the tree-green act.

Thistle, weevil, rain—whoever prays, prays.
Ever the green door opens, you must go there.

&
At Big Creek, celestial creaking—canopy-light,
world greening and the river-white sound.
I knew no lullabies but sang her a story

where in the story the horse Mazy dies—
where she would go, what hope unfolding,
what mind concluding down around her.

Forage the wet forage. Forage the dry.
She was a bit of birdsong her stubborn self—
in rule of point and passage, in point of being.

And the skinny cow-faced dog is rat now
and the grassy puddles tremble in the rain.

&
Also I penned a delicate engine, green wash over.
Saw several mysteries unfolding—*Gracie Gracie Gracie:*
barn owls in the palm tree (heads on shoulders) sleeping.

Book says *Not ever three grown owls in a single tree*!!
Three Gracies say *maybe well a PALM tree.*
Maybe not MAYBE the Gracies say,——

or why would anyone draw an engine ever now?
Where will I go with my engine, my unfolding.
In rule of great and thick, in rule of passage——

wand, prayer, deck of cards, revolver——
why would anyone ever draw an engine now?

&
If I wanted to know what the birds want
I should have paid attention to the book,
it being late in the history of study.

Still—what kind of bird would just stand there
under the sun for mad dogs, pecking at rocks
where once the birdbath sat,—bird stupid.

&
That bloody sickle is our moon, the hills are black.
The chickens have broken their own warm eggs,
the chickens have feasted on yolk.

Sleep leaves the barn owls and their phantom chicks.
Ghost-bodies speaking: this is the wind they came for.
The sound of fronds on the sky in the wind—

sound they stayed for. Body in mind-darkness.
Ministry of fog forgotten. Ministry of hunger.
Bloody sickle, hills black. The owl is stirring.

The night is a hunting night. The night is a dark door.
Ever the green door opens—*fly*.

&
Solitude of all remembrance, magnitude of knowing—
holding your muzzle I let you go down, dust—
you were a fading light then, a disappearing blaze.

Out in the open by the backhoe, Mazy
move clockwise, move counter. Moss persisting—
trough of brown water where you and the Dane drank—

murky water where the small dog swims.
Corral-dust, trough of red film settling unforgiven.
Remembering your look from a long way in.

Remembering the slow shut, then gaze returned.
Mazy leave your smell now, leave your ribbon.
Leave a plain-stay Mazy, once: your look returning.

Shut the sky darkens, shut darkens the aftermath.
With the buzzards you are not now *nowhere* circling.

&
We will calm and craze, begin another *never*.
Not the language of renewal, nor the *nothing-to-retrieve*.
For the *meant* of history lies in the seen.

Mathematics of rain on snow, for example.
Or the strategy of birds across the globe.
Or *we are not a spectator sport* say the chickens.

I brought home mustard-flower and little legumes,
small arguments home from their home in the vineyard—
for the sub-arguments of the moving mind are endless.

I let the vines cover these windows on purpose.
The bird outside is another story.

&
Chimera of shapes in neutral where the old molds break.
Chimera of things revisited will go to any length—
forgetting with remembrance at its cusp. I did it.

I did it not so long ago for unheard voices.
I did it not so long ago for scientific voices.
She was no small entrustment—I had my reasons.

The bridge and halt to later—unforgiving.
Unforgiving—the tillage in its earnest rows of clot.
The *maybe* with its next of kin the *therefore*—

land of concur and stone I am not that *I-did-it*.
Also, I am here of my own choosing.

MONEY MONEY MONEY
WATER WATER WATER

A TRILOGY

for toby and greg

Money money money
Water water water

—*Theodore Roethke, "The Lost Son"*

MONEY

Someone had the idea of getting more water
released beneath the Don Pedro Dam
into the once-green Tuolumne,——

so the minnows could have some wiggle room,
so the salmon could lunge far enough up
to spawn, so that there would be more salmon

in the more water below the dam.
But it wasn't possible—by then the water
didn't belong to the salmon anymore, by then

the water didn't even belong to the river.
The water didn't belong to the water.

THAT THE CHURCH OF ENGLAND
SHOULD BE FREE

WE APPROACH MAGNA CARTA

We approach Magna Carta from six degrees
of separation, but we approach her.
Serfs one minute, slaves the next—

and where's the shore from there?
In the interim, accounts are kept—
memories washed up to live with.

What greater claim?
What monumental difficulty—
turning law into democracy—

and then all this embedded shame.
Even the chapter on Culture Today—
that part written by some geezer

with secret ties to the monarchs.
Custom Today: sandy craters
in color, fallen walls.

All those children with no arms.
All those myths exploding.
Still, there is all manner of knowing

In the manor house—like:
Loam to be found in the quarters
where the slaves live!

+

Books of grasses books of scat
Books of rodents books of tracks
Books of sadness books of flight

How much how much where going

HUMAN OF THE FIRST FORGIVEN,

seven of the flowers,——
balancing our wages with
our ways, our unremarkable

days, (six through mist).
Thirty caves dug into
the hillside, unforgiving

repertoire of chipping. Then
ceiling-roots as new beginnings:
Then just who-so-ever,

and so-on and so-forth
all over again. Whomsoever
as the Earth's rattled

inheritance. Seedpods!
Thirty books in which
the variables were hidden:

the hybrid pelt, the edible
heirloom, etc. encircling
the lair of governance, damp

and clay-like ceiling cracking.
Thirty caves where the failures go.
Chirping under stones. Echo.

+

Smell of lavender and bay
Smell of hemispheres of thinning
Universe of years within me

Message hidden hidden nowhere

LASSITUDE AND INDEPENDENCE

The electrical plant (acres of desert)—
(we came to) and it wasn't long and we came
to the white crater of the borax plant.

The light a (post-desire) landscape (post-verdant)—
the clean bone (the sun) the day-winds (the night):
the mind gives over its small grave of secrets:

this is the way to know what you know:
determine the future history of clouds—
study (valleys) rock escarpments and canyons——.

The green world enters, introduces its yellows—
(no false reckoning, no plan, no artifice)—
the light as landscape (the specter as shore):

this is the way to know what you know:
the mind gives over its small grave of secrets——.

.

\+

Complexity of thistle and desire
Maybe a million things maybe nothing
My heart somewhere in the musty grasses

Wishes nothing who wishes stone

SOLIDS AND NON-SOLIDS

The air is solids and non-solids.
The person is solids and non-solids:
Solids and non-solids all the way down.

Halo of leaves. Aura of notes.
No kidding. All the way down.
Forgotten and not forgotten.

Candle. Matches. Needle. Down.
The old-fashioned stream remains.
The mind remains, thinking *lost*

lost, loster—all the way down.

+

Water-borne poison
Poison borne by air
Data on dead animals

Angry children on the move

COVE

*

Lithonate is some sort of lithium
and crawling is some sort of life.
I don't know how they do it elsewhere

but here we all try to be awfully good
—and still sometimes they lock us up.
Life made proper isn't what you think.

Where the woods meet the cove
there should be a sentence written in stone—
far enough back so the water can't get it,

push it around with its mindless rippling.
Meanwhile, leaves turn on their axes of air—
i.e.: it is fall: the straw-colored fields

are useless now, and the woods, too—useless,
with their loud display: if they want
anything it's to be left alone—left out

of the poem, allowed to die in peace.

+

The creation of want
The creation of debt
The creation of the toxic ponds

If they wave wave back

**

I'm no lover of human skin in any shade.
I prefer the animals who live
without their souls—how there's nothing

that floats away on a sea of sky
like a *what-did-you-say-we-were* by and by.
Hell, I don't even know what I am

right now,—a forgettable fact?
I don't know *a thing*, but I like
to hope I'll get this figuring figured—

that God will lean out of some cloud
bellowing my name, waving my ribbon.
Oh hell. Have mercy on us—

someone. Anyone. Anyone who is watching.
Save up. Save us. (*Big job.*)

+

Ditch company to sell shares
Shares of water to Audubon
For bird habitat on terms

Elsewhere offered to lettuce farmers

***

There ought to be a path with a promise—
it's a kiss with a sense of closure,
it's a graceful way to die.

If you've got something that stands
for prayer, roll it on down the road
in my direction—I'll be standing

at the rim of the patient and organized
forest, to the left of a quaking aspen.
I'll be scanning the horizon for a smudge

of myself. Roll it on down—
I like to watch things wobble.

+

A gray and helpless stringency
Bootstraps gone missing
Patterns of light on the dog

A home for the omen

****

I was raised on the enlightened consumerism
of upper bohemia, fell from grace into
lower bohemia—which is defined by

an inability to take adult responsibility:
don't sell *me* anything on credit.
In fact, don't sell me anything at all.

Thank you. Now listen here—
I took the workshop on basic functioning,
studied the universal precautions

and the diagram of the evacuation plan,
I sent away for the free booklet
on why I was born. You can trust me

with your children now—the eggs
are hidden in the bushes to signify
rebirth, bread in the oven, beans

on the stove, knife in the drawer.
To signify rebirth.

+
Rancher paid to forgo
Forgo third cutting of hay
To leave water in the streams

For late-summer fish flows

*****
I came out of the dark hills
and the dark hills own me. I have
no patience for the sticky-minded

stratums. The concern of the comfortable
for the comfortable makes me sick. Meanwhile,
the red leaves spin on their axes of air,

different leaves now, different axes,
same big death. And wouldn't we love
to shrug now and just say sorry?

Apparently not say sorry.
Let's not talk about it.
I wish I lived in an opium cloud.

+
Make way for seeing
Make way for blindness
Make way for the vision

Of sea caught in cove

******

Listen—it's all the same:
the world in the needle,
the iron in the iron-colored sky.

There's a cove in every leaf.
Don't ask *me* how it got there
but it's like our love for thin air,

the distraction of the kiss, our hope
for something beyond what we can
plainly see—the poisoned planet poisoning.

Kmart may just well be as successful
an organization as we're up to.
But if I could tell you how to live

chances are I'd get drunk instead
and turn into some kind of stand-up
comic, say *look!—the rust is unfurling*

as far as the human eye can see!

+
The greater part of the world
World upon us
Upon us the greater part

of terror

THE NARROWS

And if you cannot start
with one true thing? And if
you cannot start? If, after

the *search and rescue* paradigm
and the paradigm of *either/or,*
you are not yet perplexed

by the transport of being,—
you are at the place I call
the narrows; it is time

for a picnic in the car,
in the rain, on the cliffs
overlooking the ocean. It is

time to hear the winded
rain against the windows
and know that not far away

the ocean is in angry mourning
and that you, for all
your wind and rain, cannot

even begin to hear it.

+

Fading elasticity of spirit
In the bone-house made
I would make from this poison

House of light and birds

EXPERIENCE AS VISITATION

That which comes unwilled comes shining—
    Pulls up the sun from out dark waters,
Moves through mist, a mind in motion—
    (There is a harbor there, within you).

(Comes unwilled, comes shining)—
    Wolves lift their heads to ghost-sound,
The bird inside the box, calling—
    (Rose, birdcall, wind—come shining).

Comes of nothing, comes unbidden—
    The lunar and the mutual mission,
The mutual order and the lack—
    (Every ruptured and unclaimed fact).

That which comes unbidden comes directly—
    (Comes unleashed, uncharted and—comes shining).

+

Books of fact books of shadow
Books of poems books of prose
If you want to revisit the house of bones

Don't ask me to come with you

MAGNA CARTA

That the church of England should be free—
And have her whole rights and liberties, inviolable—
The city of London shall have her liberties and free customs—
All Archbishops, Bishops, Abbots, Priors, Templars—
Shall have their liberties and free customs—

All Hospitallers, Earls, Barons and all Persons—
As well Spiritual as well Temporal—
Shall have their free liberties and free customs—
And the cities and burroughs and towns—
And the Barons of the Five Ports and all other ports—

One measure of Wine shall be through our realm—
And one measure of Ale, and one measure of Corn—
And one breadth of dyed Cloth, that is to say—
Two Yards and it will be of Weights as it is of Measures—

+
If they wave wave back
If they falter hide
If they linger stay hidden

Stay hidden

MAYBE LATER

Who enrages maybe later—
Who watches over enrages—
Delicate Laws Of The Aftermath—

Delicate clatter: however—
However there are still children—
However the last gasp gasping *children*—

An unforgivable innocence for later—
They are a brand of aftermath—
Later we will all be equal—

Cedar fell and neutral under rain—
Nation of clatter and tremble—
Of he-who-watches-over remember—

+

Numbered keys on numbered nails
Numbered days in numbered years
Innumerable flies on the fawn the dog killed

Two dark mules in memory

MAGNIFICENT DEFENDER
OF THE AFTERMATH

knows fate's a sure device, says
it's the world of the word—therein:
not wager, not sin, fate. The dead

explore the coastlines, grays
and charcoals excluded, roots—excluded,
and the drift and moor of elsewhere

temporarily, it seems, forbidden. They
come and go, walking their circles
around us, walking out a little

into the thick of it, the thicket of
a little ice storm, a little hay-stack,—
a little nay-saying thicket. Ticket out.

+
I can't hear the whisper
I can barely feel the breath
Elsewhere gnats drinking

Drinking from the eyes of children

TINTORETTO NATIVITY
(canvas painted over, 1550s)

The angel has been chopped in half
and his legs covered over. The legs
of Christ on the cross have been
painted over. The rocks on which
the main figures sit were clouds.

—MUSEUM PLAQUE

+

Some rise up from ash as greenery
Some as a darker measure of being
Some go as water some as day

Some refuse even to say their names

TAMOXIFEN

My mother gives me her earrings—
and a ring. We sort through
shells and sand, we kneel

in salt water, we nap.
We are two women
in the shade a cliff makes.

The sun paints the water.
The wind paints the sand.
In every direction, gulls cry.

It was never a question
of what they were for—
the sand and the sea, the pearl

on the pink shell of an ear—
but they sent her back
from the eclipse and she

didn't come back. Just
as blue is an illusion
for sky, just as the wind

takes the fog out, just
how we say it: *doorless,*
doorless,—then *stay.*

+

Lost the sky within the blade
The blade within the loam
The thought within the dome of days

Lost the dome of days

VACUUM DRAMA

Or stay alive in drama of houses
and dogs,—old paintings
of cows, small fast cars,

exploding, but not before a swirl
down the twisted coastline.
And if the sea isn't the thing?

No to the steaming horizon then.
No to fear eating the life.
Flashy Gnostic suck-hole returning:

—*Hello* darling-black sunshine.
—*Hello* moon-black sunshine.
—Black flame-of-the-sun, *hello:*

the children of memory are dreams.
I'd say the sea *is* the thing.
Or the muddy grasses, the broken egg.

Or singing on the landing!
The herons have no knowledge of this—
save the narrows of the river,

the straits between the bay and ocean.
Which is, of course, the thing:
the whisper and the breathing.

All that beauty. All that dreaming.

+

Was too a story passing through
The bird outside my sister rapture
Later a house where the bees can stay

Lizard my rapture watching

DUST AND RUMBLE

No one could predict such dust and rumble.
Neither applying oneself well nor badly.
The line between us, three feet agape:

Loma Prieta or doubt——no telling.
The only break, the break as forgotten.——
I saw it in my own mind with you

on the other side as a mistake.
Who thought we could create
such dust and rumble, who thought

all we needed was a clean slate,
level ground, and a bag of marbles.
Forgotten, the only break in the break.

+

Books of names books of flowers
Books of trees books of hours
Books of dead books of living

How much less where going

FALLEN LEAF LAKE

DYING OF STUPIDITY

Dying of stupidity we want must muster something—
Nothing stepping forward, nothing forgetting:
The subsequent prying a disaster, a bloodletting.

Anaesthetizing clatter where once we carried upward—
Neither to enlarge our souls nor put the world out—
Who watches over, let us go somewhere now together.

I think there is one oak for every millionth child,
One glass of water (human or god) for every millionth child.
Neither to enrage, defend or compensate—neither nor *nor.*

What cross now bearing, what shadow throwing.
How much less where going, the object of love?
Good and Evil in quotes? How hard can it be.

+

Lamb saying flies on my eyes
Saying shit in my fur
Dark sounds caught in my throat

Her heart of fire gone now

FALLEN LEAF LAKE

—For my grandfather

And we are looking for his spirit-home.
In the dark we walk this way and that.
In the high dark mountains of fire season

we walk this way and that.

The tall pines with their rough bark
smell of brown sugar and vanilla.
The dry needles slip under our feet.

In the hot dark of fire season.
Next to the lake in the shape of a leaf.
We are looking for his spirit-home.

We are looking for his—grave, yes.

+

Cluttered lair of the forgotten
Not I the one but I the many
How much more-so where going

The object of love

THE GEESE

slicing this frozen sky know
where they are going—
and want to get there.

Their call, both strange
and familiar, calls
to the strange and familiar

heart, and the landscape
becomes the landscape
of being, which becomes

the bright silos and snowy
fields over which the nuanced
and muscular geese are calling.

+

The greater part of the season of rain
Upon us the greater part of loss
Me in my forgetfulness

You betraying matter

PROSODY

Fatso, lard-ass, pig-face, tub

is what they mostly called him
that year he failed P.E.
and religion, — the year
his mother's house burnt down

which was also the year of the flood.

Till then he'd thought of life
as a meaningful motion toward song—.

These days, if you ask him,
he'll just grin, shrug—

say *music is as music do*es.

+

This is the pod of the sweetgum
That is the floodplain
This is the housefly from hell

That is an old Chevrolet

THE MULE DEER ON THE HILLSIDE
THE RIVER DREAM
THE HISTORY

*

Where is my lover now
if not in history?

The boats are on the river
still, as I dreamed them—

and the mule deer
dip their muzzles

into the bucket and lift
them up, dripping

in the heat-smeared summer
while elsewhere

the dry grasses smoke
and crackle.

+

Then he pulled his own red cap
Over the boy's head and together
They stopped weeping

Weeping and walked on

**
John says the dead
and the living share
the same world, only

the living do not know it.
The deer we named Argonaut
lifts his mule-face

into his deer-history,
and his deer-thoughts shine:
chewing, unblinking

he considers me gravely.

+
When the birds fall out of the sky
And the fish wash up on the shore
Come and get me we'll ask for more

The use of the human body as spirit

***

The doe we named
for her fence-scars,
the doe we named

for her broken ear,
the tiny doe we named
for the white inside

her legs, along
her belly and her
twin, still spotted

fawns, lie under the oaks—
heads high, composed.
This water. *This* air.

+

While we were sleeping
The boy in the red cap exchanged
The dead bird for a living bird

Then bicycled on down the road

****

With what besides the soul
could you believe the body

has a voice? We put
the body of that rattler

on the stone pillar
by the drive, an offering

for the raptors if they'd
have her. When I went back

for the head, it clamped
my rusty shovel blade.

+

The heavens open the birds
Birds drop down from the sky
The oceans and bays deliver

Their stars and fish to the shore

*****
And there's the rattler-buzz
the mole imitates
in her panic, hands

blindly paddling the air
while Toby snaps her spine
four times, drop of blood

tipping her long nose
the way milk beaded
on the nose of the mouse

we found, still blind—
in the sun-scorched vineyard,
rowing in his darkness

for all he was worth
and not a nest in sight.
Where is my lover's body now

if not in history, in sky,
in the scent of vinegar grass
and the dry-smelling chaparral.

+

Do you remember our little boat
The father said to his boy
On the bed—the boy's mind

Thus occupied he died

THE GIFT

Whether you think of life
as gates and bridges, or traps
in the form of doors

left open; whether you
are waiting for the snap
of neck, or for the arc

of light—by which to measure
your horizon (caper of particles
and motion); whether you know

or not that the great
enthrallment may or may not
be coming: death says

listen for the echo. Begin
with thunderstorms and move
slowly toward the calm wherein

white trumpets of amaryllis
sag in the sticky dusk—
listen for the soundtrack

of the echo in the weather.

+

Unruffled un-trusted unheard
Unheard from sea-marsh unfailing beach
Undeveloped seedpods unhoused

I come unhoused

SPIRIT'S

got a stone around its noose,—
goodbye to *maybe*, goodbye
to *artifact* and *challenge*.

Artifice and *act* reviving.
Noose coming up empty. Net
coming up empty. Spirit's

not a stone, but a noose
releasing. Daemon's
a death-wish rethinking. Me?

I am neither here nor elsewhere,—
abandoned unto utter abandon.

+

Their laughter was their only own land
Once you start carrying your wounded
Wounded it's a different story

A mute pretending after another elsewhere

INCOMPLETE SCENARIO
INVOLVING FIRE AND WATER

Authority: off
somewhere in the dark
wings, conducting terror.

The smart daughter,
too—off in the wings
with her startling

ineptitude and her shame.
The strong daughter alone
is doing well though

she has neglected
her patrol—how else explain
the house, in flames.

And how explain
what keeps you
from going the way

of the dining-room table,
that gorgeous
inferno, but to mention

the white husky.
Who that white dog?
And *where* the shimmering

over the bay of clear sailing?

+

In a remote and steamy ocean
I lost my mother
She is not haze not mist

She is that pure

THE BIRD THAT KEEPS
THE SLOW BOY SPINNING

The bird that keeps
the slow boy spinning—
is extinct: though the boy

with the chapped face
crosses our streets, though
it is *our* spattered fenders

that hit him, he is
listening to the bird from
the other landscape, the bird

that never arrives—
the way we keep circling
long after we die.

+

Looking for a gravesite
Hoping for a major notion
Watercress ditch-side

Where the old spring fades

THE ELEPHANTS IN THE OCHRE CLAY

The ochre elephants
did not fail me,—I failed
to meet them half way.

Therefore I cannot envision
them entire, just trunks
in ochre sway: an inhuman

account of beauty, a pattern
for the oceans to pick up on
and with which the wind might play.

+

Wisdom you've forgotten
Garden of wisdom we've forgotten
The bird in yesterday

Almost the bird in tomorrow

WALKING, BLUES

Rain so dark I
can't get through—
train going by

in a hurry. The voice
said *walk or die*, I
walked,—the train

and the voice all
blurry. I walked with
my bones and my heart

of chalk, not even
a splintered notion:
days of thought, nights

of worry,—lonesome
train in a hurry.

+
Going to town for vodka at noon
Turning the ghost away
The heart a lump of meat

Meat in its nest of fluid

WE GO FROM LIGHT INTO DARKNESS
WITH BARELY A WORD TO SAY

Despair, that wash
of nightmare—
returning: if it

does not kill
you, you will
come to the day

when a crow makes
a vision of the
lemon tree—kind

of moment you'd
give a life for—
(Just see to it

that it does
not kill you.)

+

Now as animal bodies
As the glistening fur
Fur in the rain smells

Let us smell

STALKING THE PLEASURES

The pleasures are the *can-be*
and the *want*, the abundance
of water before the well

went dry. The pleasures
are primitive stalks of *might-be*
and *aftermath*, shaded

and bamboo-like grasses
on the arduous walk
to the waterfall: first

brush so thick we crawl,
then down into the dense
and muggy grasses, muddy

elbows and no idea where
the path is—stalking
the pleasures: *heart-beat*

can-be, stone's-throw, want.

+

There was only one egg
One hard-boiled egg
And Akhmatova

Gave it to Mandelstam

DOROTHY PRETENDING
TO BE WATER

DOROTHY PRETENDING
TO BE SKY

THE LENGTH OF LIFE

*

There is the risk of touching and shrieking.
(There is mist on the pond,—so I watch it.)

I know I should be elsewhere, talking.
(Everyone else is elsewhere, talking.)

Mostly, they talk about touching and shrieking.
Sometimes it's oysters and snowmobiles.

+

The European grapevine moth task force
Recommends the deployment
Of mating disruption pheromone products

Products prior to the first flight

**

A thought rocked me gently to sleep once.
(Not a truth, but a universe.)

Then there was shrieking, and I lost it for always.
Years later, I asked my sleep to guide me.

The way was found to be quicksand
and the surrounding light—was blinding.

+

First generation flights begin
Near bud-break adults live
One to three weeks

Fly at dusk mate in flight

***

Mist on the pond where a scene is missing.
This is the forward-marching of history?

(The air that holds the mist is real.)
(Science says the mist is real.)

(The myth of history outlives science.)
Probably, I should be elsewhere—talking.

+

Infested clusters shrivel
Fully excavated berries dry
Fungal invaders are present

Last males trickling in

****
The girl in the tunic passes raw tuna—.
The guests all agree: the ocean is true.

The men are experts on parts of real oysters.
The women are experts in drawing the parts.

(Mother drew them to scale with an ivory ruler.)
Counties of color—in black and white.

+
7 May conventional insecticides
Continue to hold up well Altacor
Dipel Lannate Intrepid Brigade

Delegate Renounce Entrust Success

*****
Later, the way was found to be quicksand.
(Read history, read water, read pond—read myth.)

I told this first as The History Of Dark Waters.
(There was plenty of touching and plenty of shrieking.)

I offer it to you as comedy.
(I lost the one friend who knew it was funny.)

+

Timing and treatment of third flight
Of European grapevine moth is pending
The red dirt avenues the gibbous moon

I waver burdensome re spraying

******

There is always the risk of shrieking and lightning.
The way may be found to be quicksand or sight.

My mother gave me an ivory ruler.
My father gave me a labyrinth to live by.

The way may be found to be myth, to be history,——.
(Mist on the pond, where the scene is missing.)

+

Larva samples at ag office
Weight tags at department of weights
As in department of weights and measures

As in Bureau of Water Reclamation

LIKE A BLIND MAN
I CROUCH DOWN

My mother pots or doesn't pot the soil.
In the cold rain, I crouch down.
My ears are clean, but there's a boil
on my elbow and soil
under my nails, crusty and blood-brown.

December rains gather, froth and boil—
the river runs brown with topsoil.
On the road the earthworms stretch and drown.
(My ears are clean but there's a boil
where my heart should be and soil
in the flashing waterfalls near town.
My lover tilled or didn't till that soil.)

Loyal, disloyal, loyal, disloyal,
loyal. I flip my penny to the ground.
My forehead's mud-streaked. There's a boil
where the icy waters rise and roil.

In the field, the field-mice drown.
My brother loves or doesn't love the soil.
In the field the narrow ditches boil.

+

The story of a place is a crooked story
The story of a family is worse
In the valley a thousand lights

And every light a failure

FROM THE FAMOUS CASTLE
OF NONEXISTENCE

*
I looked up one day
and saw my father creating
his soul by loving

the souls of trees.
It became easy then
to look for yellow

in the woods—easy
to call that looking
faithful to all things.

+
So what was the best way
What the way without I
Green pods of the walnut tree

Spiked and overhead

**

On the second day
the yellow dogs
come out of the woods

to play with me and Alice—
they surprise us. After that
there is a smallness in us

within which we are waiting.

+

Down Toby's trail to the burr-filled meadow
Up Alice's burr-filled trail to the ridge
Toby and Alice as dogs when we leave

On our return—Toby and Alice as bushes

MOWING AND AFTERMATH

Shock of rocks on the metal blades now:
(We left the corral gate open.
We let the weeds grow high.)

The orange falls into the house finch nest.
Small dog skips up the vineyard:
Reptiles and rodents to demolish, demolished!!

The lesser hope is the greater burden.
I could not my own fool life abandon.
No sun, no moon, no mowing?

No mustard disked under for mustard gas?
Turtles all the way down writes the monk.
And what kind of support system is *that.*

+

The world full of tractors
Is the mystery world
The other world

Is the seasons

STILL LIFE AND
STILL LIVING

*

Cabernet to the right.
Zinfandel to the left.
Slope and tilt of

the red road through
the north vineyard—
quirky passage I've been

for fifty years, where now
the girl-dog Alice
and the vineyard-master

Ramon are circling our best
tractor as if it were
a philosophical problem.

+

Three a ton or five an acre
He pulls leaves he drops fruit
Five a ton or eight an acre

We pull leaves we drop fruit

**

The turtle at the willows
doesn't know: water
table dropping, water

hole shrinking every
year where the wild
rhododendron bloom.

In that tiny whorl of
her thought—there's
barely enough mist

to get lost in—
so she keeps bumping along
as if there were no

problem: for she is one
of the sturdier gifts
on this mission.

+

He sells his handshake he breaks his word
He sputters over his sputtering jet
He thinks I'm a girl and can't do math

And he can kiss my lily-white ass

TOBY THE STRAY

The crown of his head smelled of redwood boughs
where he wiped his eyes in the morning.
The bottom of his feet smelled like brown sugar.

Through summer grasses, through winter fog
we set our compass on his white tail, waving.
The crown of his head smelled of redwood boughs.

He tipped his nose into the breeze, took his readings,
thanked me for dinner, snoozed on his back. Happiness
was his calling, and his feet smelled like brown sugar.

Close in the night, the coyotes fell silent
when he loosed his deep bark. There was a white heart
on the crown of his head. (It smelled of redwood boughs.)

He survived: scorpions, rattler bite, hound paralysis
and tick fever (twice). He showed me where my heart is,
and the bottom of his feet smelled like brown sugar.

He squeaked when he yawned, he sighed when he slept—
our bear, our lion, our soft-eyed prince.
The crown of his head smelled of redwood boughs
and the bottom of his feet like brown sugar.

+

Dream of patterns of light on the dog
Several omissions missing
And somewhere still a willow

By a well that marked a grave

BIG OR SMALL WITH LANGUAGE—

the seasons heave along is how
the seasons are heaving. Sun
on the reddening grape leaves

is sun on the red-leaf virus.
Take it. Knot in the oak
where the wasps stay, upturned

bucket by the old barn, a toad-castle
for the doughy blinker with his
one fast pulsing chin. I give you

the scorpion's scuttling shadow
in moonlight—the rattler
stretched long on the warm drive

at dusk: people love images and I
want some of that love for myself.
In the clouds a nest is forming.

The barn is faded red, barn-red
and mossy. The rattler, Mojave
rattler-gray and dusty. The heart

unravels—big or small with language
doesn't the heart unravel.

+

The dream-door darkens
The world repeals itself
The dark participants repeal

The air is lavish with moisture

THE DOWN AND DIRTY KEEP-AWAY GAME
FOR THE EATEN OR JUST MISSING

I am listening for the souls of foxes

    —Down and dirty

Foxes I knew, then gone one day

    —Eaten or just missing

They leapt and played one dawn

    —whom we named Jane and Greg

They pounced on mice, nibbled seed

    —shake rattle and roll

The cat along that limb's a lion

    —eaten or just missing

Palace of light and branches

    —leaping foxes summer dawn

In the greenhouse bedroom where love began

    —began.

+
Here the doe-faced dog
Here the fawn the Dane killed
Here my father's ashes

In the bone-dry field

A SONG FOR ALICE
IN THE RAINY SEASON

You will not go to a watery grave,
You will not go to your grave with ticks—
But you will go to your grave today.

Little dog who would never behave,
Who heard us call and watched, transfixed—
You will not go to a watery grave.

To the sheep you were a blurred crime-wave,
(Puzzled by dogs who chased after sticks)—
And spirited off to your grave today.

You led the other dogs astray,
Woke the neighbors, killed their chicks—
But you will not go to a watery grave.

Before we make your nest of hay
We line the flooded pit with bricks—
For you will go to your grave today.

We line the hay with twigs of bay.
I brush your tail. I check for ticks.
You will not go to a watery grave—
But you *will* go to your grave today.

+

Tadpoles on the flats
Vernal pools shrinking
Rocks we balanced on returning

We were a story passing through

BEEN A GRAPEVINE IN MY STEAD

In the end you *are*
and then after some time
you *are not*, more or less—

as the saying goes. What
did you want? You
who were barely honored

with birth in the first
place, who nearly missed
being in this world, *you*

when there could have been
a grapevine in your stead?

+

Tug and swoop of the grape-hook
Blade a thumbnail moon
Yellow-jackets on the sticky fruit

With or without worship——truth

DOROTHY AND JANE IN TESUQUE

Dorothy pretending to be water.
Dorothy pretending to be
sky. In the wide arroyo

under cottonwoods. With electrical
lines and without. With Forgiveness
and without. We were girls—

we were beautiful children.
For good measure, we stole apples.
We cut strands of barbed wire

for our ponies' passage. The prow,
when there was a prow, cut through
green waters of the Indian

reservoirs where heron stopped
in spring. Sometimes the dream-mask
shifted: bone-bruise and blood-clot,

seepage. The cliffs were red clay—
folds of shadow and light, home
to small rodents. Mystery

with neither name nor notice,
brackish river, world of salt
cedar, a rot-out tree, bee-nested.

Now, pour the honey down my throat—
thistle-ditch of darkness, dream-door
to the sun: ours, the pit and sink

to nowhere. And nowhere my blind body.

+
Magnificent defender of skies
Magnificent defender of oceans
How much can you subtract now

How much and still get by

WORLD OF MADE AND UNMADE

Nancy Morgan Whitaker—

in memoriam

1.

...

The third time my mother fell
she stopped saying she wanted to die.

Saying you want to die
is one thing, she pointed out,
but dying is quite another.

And then she went to bed.

...

Outside her window the trees
of her orchard are heavy
with their load of ripening pecans.

The shadow of the Organ Mountains
creeps across the land,
and the blue heron stands on the shore
of the shrunken Rio Grande.

Wichita, Chickasaw, Wichita, Shoshoni:
her every tree, her every row.

—Rincon, NM, July 15

...

I bring her coffee and a bun,
and a linen napkin, but—
Jesus Haploid Christ,

as her grandfather the geneticist
would say, I mean how many
linen napkins does one person need?

How many linen napkins
the size of small tablecloths
does one person need— *LVS*

embroidered on each corner, and who
was LVS anyway?

. . .

Well, let's see, my mother begins, *LVS,*
Lilian Vaughan Sampson, would have been
your great-grandmother, the name

going back to an orphan, a boy
who took his sister's married name,
becoming Sampson in the ship's log. . .

and in this way we lost track
of that side of the family.

. . .

In the hills above Rincon
a woman is leaving jugs of fresh water
outside the Rincon Water Works

before locking the metal doors.

Rincon, where the Rio Grande
turns back on itself—
like the crook of an arm

before heading south to become
Rio Bravo del Norte. Rincon, a stop
for water on the journey north.

. . .

The United States of America
Does not extend refugee status

To Mexicans.

…

And when there was nothing left
for her to do but die,
I brought my mother home with me.

I put her in the stone cabin
by the vineyard, cabin of her X
and now dead husband, my father,

cabin he called The Fortress
in those years *his* mother
came to live there. Came to die.

...

With the mediocre portraits
of her three children
hung at the foot of her bed,

I tried to joke that she now
was trapped into looking
at our heads. And, trapped thusly,

she did what nobody
could have predicted:

she developed a sense of humor.
An emergency sense of humor.

That dark room in which
we finally spoke.

. . .

Remember how you wouldn't give up
your tonsils? All those years they floated
in formaldehyde? She's sitting in bed

with impeccable posture. Dots of blood
speckle the back of her cotton nightgown.
Her laugh now sounds like her mother's laugh—

a high crooning. And I'm remembering Cheracol—
the sticky bottle of red cough syrup,
my sticky hands, the swelling vapor-love of codeine,

and then my tonsils, sloughing all those years
in their baby-food jar, how I'd shake them—
my own private snow globe.

. . .

And with her impeccable posture
she kept her impeccable accounts
of life as we know it:

DATE 19 86	ITEMS	FOLIO	✓	DEBITS	CREDITS	BALANCE
1/31/86	TRACTOR OVERHAUL	CD1		826 10		
2/28/86	TRACTOR OVERHAUL	CD2		3144 54		
3/31/86	TRACTOR OVERHAUL			54 63		
2/28/86	BLADE	CD2		450 —		
4/30/86	14 FOOT MOWER	CD4		1028 75		4904 02
12/31/86		AJE(41)			4904 02	0 —

2.

. . .
We are lying in the big bed
and she says, *Are things between us good?*
—Yes Mom, things between us

are good.
Don't you think? I say.

No.

—No? You don't think things
between us are good?

No.

—No? Then tell me Mom,
tell me and we'll talk about it.

No.

—No? You won't tell me?

No.

. . .
Behind the filing cabinet
in my office, a mouse

begins its three-day-rot.

...
In animal darkness, before
the first day of harvest,
I walk up the vineyard's main avenue—

thumbnail moon, and the floodlight
from the big barn. Clanks and shouts.

The squat stone structures of the homestead
vanish, its layers of ghosts flicker
and go out. The black dog Leo follows me—

almost invisible when I look back:
he floats,—a low-lying, uncomplaining
black cloud. *Day by day,* I hum—

to the dog and the moon and the vineyard,
I guess,—*Let me see you more clearly*.

Love is a ticket, whatever love is.
And to where I could not say.

...

I bring breakfast, balancing the tray
across the gravel to her cabin:
the evil eye. I bring fresh sheets:

the evil eye. I mortar and pestle
the methadone: *Big* Evil Eye.

I pull morphine into the syringe.

I would like a nurse, my mother says,
who can tell the difference
between a living body and a dead one.

...

Hospice wants to interview the patient.

But the patient says
I'm deaf and I'm blind and I'm not
answering any more questions.

(The patient exaggerates.)

. . .

Turns out Leo is one lying
thieving son-of-a-bitch pooch—

coming into my office with a spot
of paper towel stuck to his lip

just before Silvia comes in to ask
about her missing sandwich.

We take the bright spots we need,
Silvia and Leo and I.

Then the laundry room floods—
then we wring out the sheets.

. . .
Somewhere in New Mexico
the house that is always cracking
continues to crack.—

Somewhere in Mexico a father
pays half the ransom and gets
half his daughter's body back.

...

The family inundates—
The talkers talk—
The dishes crack and break—

The family inundates—

Peter has lost his darts
In the gravel by the porch—
And tied his knife to the broom handle—

The talkers talk—

My mother smiles and watches—
With those blue crystal eyes
My mother drinks it all in.

. . .

How will you spend your courage,
her life asks my life.

No courage spent of—
bloodshot/gunshot/taproot/eye.

How will you spend
your courage, how

will you spend your life.

Bloodshot, gunshot, taproot, eye—
and the mind
on its slow push through the world—

...

The tumor on my mother's liver
grows fast. When she lies on her back
it's as if there were a plank

and a grapefruit under the covers.
It presses on her stomach, her bladder,
her lungs. It presses on her liver,

cuts off the bile. I try to imagine.

Hospice says, basically,——
be aware:

one day she may simply explode.
Blood from her mouth and nose.

But she will not feel a thing!

...

My mother says
I hope we are in some proximity
to the old Palo Alto Clinic.

—Yes, I say.

But not in time.
Not in space.

3.

. . .

The finest strand of deep blue yarn
connects me to my mother, spool—
unspooling.

. . .
This year I have disappeared
from the harvest routine—

the pickers throwing their trays
under the vines, grape hooks
flying, the heavy bunches flying—

pickers running to the running tractors
with trays held high above their heads
and the arc of dark fruit

falling heavily into the half-ton bins.

The hornets swarming in the diesel-filled air.

. . .

The hornets swarm in the diesel-filled air.

Wagons of grapes bump along
behind the tractor, the tractor
speeds to the concrete loading slab.

Joel backs and fills, slowly places
each bin on the truck with intense
precision—the makeshift tines

of our "forklift" slipped
onto the bucket of the backhoe.

From my mother's cabin I hear
the exhausted crews come in,
stream down the vineyard road—

their shouts distant and nearing.
And when they pass the cabin—
Viva los Estados Unidos.

…

How will you spend your courage,
Her life asks my life.

No courage spent of
bloodshot / gunshot / taproot / eye—

How will you make your way?

Then, *respond to the day*
some other way than blind—

473

...

From my mother's cabin I hear them—
Viva los Estados Unidos.

This year I haven't picked figs
or taken them sun-warm to the barn

or left them in the big tin bowl
where the flags of the US and Mexico
hang high in the rafters, left them

with the little sign: *Viva Mexico*—.

This year—

I haven't balanced on the wagon
picking bad fruit from the two bins,

or walked behind the pickers with my bucket,
or watched the bins being strapped
on the trucks, cinched down—

my white hands
fruit-sticky at my sides.

This year
I have disappeared.

Or I was never there.
Or I was never here.

...
Mexico is a snake eating
its tail, Mexico,—the fathers
shooting each other's sons, the sons

shooting each other's fathers, bodies
hung like flags from bridges,
as in the papers,

but not just in the papers—

home home home. The pastel
house on the river, salt cedar—
viva viva viva. Mexico

is a house on fire.

Miedo en todas partes.
Fear everywhere.

...
When this is all over
Ramon and Silvia say

we will take you to visit our home.

One day, they say, *we will take you
to Michoacán, from where we come.*

...

My mother's curled up on the big bed—
under the quilt like a purple sky—
big white circles for moons—.

I barely exist,
she tells me sweetly, *but you*
are not here. Then,

Shall I turn the heat down when I leave?

...

I want to press my body
all along her body—
hold her damp back to me.

. . .

The mouse behind the filing cabinet
isn't a mouse at all, but a rat or maybe

a chipmunk dead behind the wall—
and starting the long haul into bone-dom.

I move my papers to the dining room,
——the drafts of contracts, the permits,
——the white binder of death instructions.

The little white flags of prescriptions.

...
In my father's big bed
we lie face to face
and tangle our hands together.

They are almost identical
almost inseparable.

When I was young, she drew the fish
for his publications—

then he started disappearing for days
with Timothy Leary, and just like that
she stopped—and gave me her ivory ruler.

I untangle myself
and go for her morphine.

...
This is one of her fish:

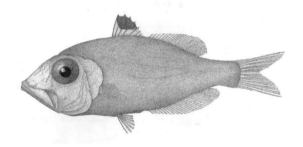

...
This is another:

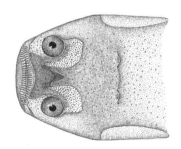

...

In my father's lab the aisles were narrow
the shelves were high, jars and jars:
the egg, the embryo, the adult male,

the adult female,—ocean species
of every kind staring out at us
from their sea of formaldehyde.

Octopuses and squid, my favorites—
eyes closed, eyes open, tentacles
curled out against the jar, tentacles

curled in. All that perfection.
World of made and unmade.

...

In my dream my mother comes with me.

We are in the meadows we call
The Flats, walking the dogs.

Walk straight past the water trough,
she says, *do not engage the moss.*

Go back to the top of the page,
the dream says, and leave out the suicides.

In my dream I walk and walk.

After a time—no mother.
After a time—no dogs.

Just the field of dry grasses
and me and the walking.

Then just the walking.

. . .

Yes dear—I would like some wine.

It's what I have to give—
dark fruit of the rocky soil.

Sorry to leave—oh, I'm really
sorry to be leaving.

Sticky tumbler, sticky straw.

. . .

—Would you like to go to sleep now?
Yes, but only temporarily.

...

Is that MY black dog—
with telltale compost on his nose?
Blade of grass, squash of persimmon,

some leggy insect on his forehead
next to the growth? Is that MY
red truck speeding up the vineyard's

central avenue, porta potty
bumping along behind, toilet paper
unfurling behind in celebratory loops?

...

We are sitting on the side of the bed.
What are you doing? she says—

—I'm giving you the evil eye.
You keep giving me the evil eye
and now I'm giving it back.

We laugh.

Oh. And what is this?

Those are my hands, Mom.

...

My mother takes my two hands
in her two hands and pulls herself
up to standing.

It is time, she says.

You know what to do, she says.

Do it tonight. My wishes,

while I still have wishes.

...

Rain, and the grape sugars
are dropping.

The phone has gone out.

...

Passing back to the house
from my mother's cabin
in the full-moon light:

her wheelchair tracks in the gravel
make a wide turn and disappear
into the shadow of the palm tree,

as narrow-gauge tracks disappear
into the deep mine shafts
of the Sierra Nevada.

In the house, the dogs
are pacing back and forth
behind the window.

. . .
At night I go for a personal best:
Law & Order: Special Victims Unit,
season 8, episodes 9-12. By day,

the grapes come in: October 10,
6 tons Zinfandel; October 16,
34 tons Cabernet; season 9

episodes 1-5. You get the picture.

My mother, in particular, would like
to get the long process of her departure
from this planet over with.

...

The finest strand of deep blue yarn—
spool unspooling.

6.

...
My mother's every exhale is
somewhere between a rasp
and a scream now.

Hospice says they'll bring
phenobarbital in the morning.

Between us we have
—new bottle of morphine
—the dog's phenobarbital
—three syringes of Parry's insulin
—methadone, Haldol, etc.

Parry and I discuss combinations.
We want the best for our mother.

We do not want
to fuck this
one up.

       — October 22, +/- 2 a.m.

...
On the phone, my brother Whit
says *Don't Google it*.

...
+/- 3 a.m.

Parry sits up straight, says, *but*
how can we kill our own mother?

How can we kill our own mother?

—We cannot. No.
No we cannot
kill our own mother.

...

So we measure the morphine carefully
with a syringe and administer it
every five minutes, as instructed,
forcing it between her gluey lips.

We no longer speak—we
no longer look at one another.

...

(My mother's every exhale is
somewhere between a rasp
and a scream.)

. . .

Ben! Oh, Ben,
Oh Ben, Ben
my mother cries—

anguish all over
again for the dog
with the wolf's mouth

who kept her going
as long as he
could keep going.

Then *Mitch, Mitch*
for her grandson,

Stay away from the water.

...
Now my mother's every exhale
is a scratchy scream.

Parry is trying to get through—
she says what it says
to say in the white binder:

Mom, let go—Mom!

But my mother's heart
is a strong heart.

...
I myself do what I do best:
I get under the covers with my mother
and hold a pillow over my head.

...

Just after seven we turned her
on her side to pour out
the watery phlegm—

and when we turned her over again
she had begun her dying.

...

The life falls shut,
the life falls shut
slowly. So slowly.

—Napa, CA, October 22

. . .
The day after my mother died
we finished the grape harvest
and the day after that
Ramon and Joel and Ruben

began spreading hay
on the avenues. Nobody
really spoke much.

There were little red dots
like fire, that were not fire,
on the hills across the bay.

...
She died on her 84th birthday
about which she had this to say
to herself, albeit two days early:

Happy Birthday on the very day,
and all the usual pleasantries.

...
—The never the over the void
ever the gone gone...

She always did what she wanted to do.
She ate her beans with a silver spoon.

She gave me my steely blue.

. . .
Silvia asks whether I ever feel
my mother's presence, the way we do
sometimes with the dead, who can

make themselves felt, who can feel a lot
like the speechless living when they want to,
—as when that great horned owl

stared at me from the deodar tree
while I was thinning radishes—until
I looked up and saw her glaring

and, not knowing what else to do, waved.

Truth is, I do not feel my mother's presence.
Truth is, if ever a person were to fail

to become a disembodied presence it would be

my beautiful and practical mother.

...

Her ashes blow off—
grit on the cold wind—
through her orchard, 2001

pecan trees, about which
she wrote me once
from what some considered

her self-exile down
by the Mexican border—
I don't know why

it gives me such pleasure
to cause 2001 living things
to thrive, but it does.

Back then, her new trees stood
just three feet high. She
pruned them standing and carried

her entire harvest around
in a briefcase, looking
for future buyers.

—Rincon, NM, November 19

...

Rincon, where the Rio Grande turns
back on itself before heading south
to become Rio Bravo del Norte. Rincon,

a stop on the long journey to The North—
where demand for water runs so high
that by the time it reaches Mexico

the river sometimes runs dry.

. . .

And the bit about the answer
blowing in the wind—
what does it mean?

As a flag blows?
A leaf downed? A leaf hanging?

Or like a piece of grit
when the last thing in the world you need
is grit in the eye?

. . .

Because elsewhere in this valley
working in an orchard is the man
from Mexico—who on the eve

of his daughter's quinceañera
was able to pay only half her ransom.

Can no amount of squinting bring this
into full view of the life-size heart?

. . .

In the phone photograph
of us in the orchard now,
Parry holds a tin pitcher

with our mother's ashes
and we three look small,
wizened almost, in our grief.

The trees, formidable
and orderly are losing
their leaves. The pecans

pop out of their casings—
ready for their winter harvest.

Wichita, Chickasaw, Wichita, Shoshoni:
her every tree, her every row.

Nancy Morgan Whitaker
October 22, 1929—October 22, 2013

NEW POEMS

THE WORLD PER SE

It was a story most like any other
and might have stayed that way were it not
for minor disturbances in the fabric of thought

and then the tearing in the fabric of the brain.
For this was the world per se.

+

Was there, one might ask, *not*, for example,
some counter-story the shivering
rabbits would have told

(perhaps about how fear can come and go)
were there wavelength and receiver to be had.

No? Was there not?

+

Their tracks in the snow hugged the hedge
so that was where I put the apples,
but this isn't the kind of thing I'm counting.

The history of man is the history of animals:
door to the spirit world, meat-machine
in a cramped dark space. What *is* pain

but an impulse in the nerves?

All I can say is *beware*—
and who needs a wavelength for that?

+

I was twelve and he was drunk,
I was driving and he was coaching,
the day I almost killed my father.

The sound of a man with his boot trapped
between the wheel of a tractor and its body
is the scream of a terrified pig.

The sound of botched slaughter.

His tractor, my tractor now.

+

Do we ever really go beyond the story
we were born to—

do we?

As the blind do
because they must?

Do we ever *really* have
a self to go home to?

+
The torn river,
the tattered sky,
that summer played back in the mind:

down by the river the lightning bugs
alarmed, or *not-alarmed-and-resting.*

Today, in the shallows made of melted ice
the walleye swim toward the hook,

the gray fox finally chews
her paw all the way off
and leaves it behind in the trap,

and the black colt frisks in the snow.

(Hook and trap aside now
some other language calling.)

\+

Once I dreamed a white coyote
lived under my porch
but it was only dreaming

(and only a porch)—
still, counterpoint for
the heart has no say in the matter,

the white coyote has no say.

I fed the rabbits apples,
admired the patterns their tracks made in the snow.

+

In the book on factory farming
the boy from the slaughterhouse explains
how something comes over you on the floor,

"so that, once, when the pig looked up at me,
I just reached out and sliced his snout off.

First that poor thing turned in circles
with a terrible shrieking, but after a while
he just sat down and looked at me stupidly."

+

There was a fox I saw once—
before she started her chewing.

When I startled her out of hiding
she dragged the rusted trap
up and over the stone wall—

and it weighing at very least
ten times what she did.

By the time I came back
with my leather gloves
she was, of course, gone—

the low sun was staining
the golden flats
a deeper shade of gold

and that was that.

+
There ought to be a law
against this kind of trapping—

and there is.

There is *always* a law.

How can it be
that after all these years

I still have no idea
how to live.

+

Years ago my father gave me the buffalo hide
his father's father used to survive
one winter, as story would have it.

I put its scratchy tangle on my bed.
Nothing in that night sounded familiar

and in the morning,—I felt
hunted of a sudden then.

+

By the time I came back with gloves, of course
she was gone. By the time I came back, with gloves,
of course she was gone. Of course she was gone

by the time I came back with gloves.

+
The wind runs high.

The mangled animals seem like the heart
but they are not the heart.
Their living and their dying belong to them.

We can wear that decay straight ahead,

or count birds, make a little True
from sticks and lichen, a little Echo
of summer played back in the mind—

turn ourselves over to the love of animals,
the deep Guernsey River or the flaking ice
at the edges of the Yellow Jack Creek,

but this storm isn't dreaming
and beauty is worth *what* compared to wool now.

+

Therein lies the poverty of logic.
Therein lies the poverty of truth.

+
Where does the world *go*
when the hungry goldfinches flitting
on the frozen twiggy limbs of the lilac
like electrified buds—

"take your breath away,"
and you fly out of your life.

Where does the world go
and what's that other world
that will not keep us?

+
Sibley says the ovenbird
makes her nest like a cup on the ground—

capped with a dome of grass and leaves.

The cowbird lays her eggs
in the nests of other birds
which tend the cowbird young

"often at the expense of their own"

while the "noisy and aggressive" blue jay
simply eats the eggs of other birds.

But this is all I'm sure of—that summer
my dog Toby ate the quail eggs
out of their nest on the ridge,

two birds returned, loud
in their looking and looking.

+

In their broken pot by the shed—
stiff and upright in the sideways snow,

the dead marigolds quiver.

Comes the moment when you cannot see
for all that fury on the gentle snow.

+

(Comes a moment
when you see as the crow sees—

your body as slaughterhouse,
as beggar on the flat world, kneeling.)

+

After my father died
I found seven deer hearts in his freezer—*seven*.
Hoarded tariff from the hunters on his land—

frozen, when everybody knows
the first thing you eat is the heart.

A GOOD MOON

As is the name of the earth, goes this good one.
As is the name of the molten river.
As is the name, that river going forth.

The moon in the trees was a good moon,
the world in the sound bite, a good world.
As in tunneling, the years went forth.

Narrow misses. Some bright star for stopping.

Madeleine gave me pomegranate seeds.
Betsey gave me strong tea with sugar.
Already we have suffered over the dropped fruit enough.

Already we have drunk the wine and suffered.

I have not yet come to a place of stopping.
You have not yet come to a place of stopping.
This is the way. Some people have hands.

Being a woman, you flow and keep.
There's a birthing-tent waiting on the plains.
This is the way. Some people have hands.

BARBED WIRE

After all, why *should* one gringo
have all the apples—

with her Spanish-dancer skirt billowing,
her bellowing, and her waving around of arms?
And the apples softening into the grass.

And why should The Wire That Made The West
not make way for one hungry pony
and two skinny girls

with a pair of wire-clippers.

BLUE VISION

It could have been ocean.
It could have been sea.
It could even have been sky.

I didn't know I was dreaming.

There might have been birds.
They might have been shadows of birds.
After all, it was dreaming.

Sweat on my body, sun on my sleep.
I thought the satiny field was water.
Either way, there were dream-gulls.

Either way, the homecoming gray:
waking between sea and sky
with the one note over and over keening.

BOUNTY

of my body where skin meets air,
great are the voices.

When will you go there?
How can I finish the poem

if you do not touch me?

Who will linger?
Who will pull the trigger.

Or the roiling in the pearl sky
and the pink-brown ocean

name me?

THE OUTSTRETCHED EARTH

Do you know what whole fields are?
They are fields with a dog and a moon.
Do you know the answer—for the many?

Except there would be vineyards.
Meaning there would, as usual, be commerce.
Money, and a game of sorts to play it.

Meanwhile—Emma lost in the cover-crop.
Top of her head bobbing through mustard flower.
It is, after all, still here—

the real world, the outstretched earth,
rain, soil, copper for pennies.

THE WATERFALL OFF ATLAS PEAK ROAD

The rock's high place is now—
Then the water then the tumble—
The rocky draw, the waterfall—

The canyon into which that boy jumped—
Jumped from where the water flies—
Flies off the lip of the rocky draw—

Fans out through air all winter—
For the long drop into the canyon—
Into which the lonely boy jumped—

Jumped from the rock's high place—
Is a *now* and a *now* and a *now*—

IF MY MOTHER WERE ME
NEITHER WOULD SHE

have had children:
one strummed chord's
un-strumming, one inscape

lying low. The rest is
all landscape: all *birth*
and *hag*, all *hill*

and *hollow*. Shoot
and soil laid bare
by the no-one and the not-

watching. And this is
for sure me, inviting
you home mother,——inviting.

LUCK

In the system of pulleys and chains
we find our life's work.
As they call it. Pulleys

as they call them. Chains.
Our life's work. Our calling.

ANNIE MARCHES TO WORK
16 BELOW

I didn't even bother
trying to start the car.

One frozen icicle
on my lashes was

the only issue.
Hard to see

through the icicle.

ANNIE THE JEWELER
DESCRIBES HER KIDNEY STONE

10 mm, size
of a 2.5 carat diamond.

THE DEODAR TREE IN THE PRESENT

Her dreams were
shaking his
home apart—.

She left him
with the quilt she sewed
in the ladder pattern,

color of moss
and snow. If
you want to know—

she's swinging on
the swing swung
off the branch

of the old deodar.

JOHN'S DOG KING
AND HIS LITTLE BAND
OF EMBATTLED HOMELESS

The dog King
would lead them
to safety, even

if he could do it
only in his mind—
in his mind

he would lead them
all to safety.

HE

+

Out of quarry-dust
he comes running.
Running as a crab runs,

he comes out of the hills
the hills that own him—
as a lie comes to own

its person, like that.
And the hackles of the land
rise up behind him.

+

On the sub-zero
rangeland the deer
bed down. He—

harrowed, and holds
rivers of snow
and forgetting—he

beds down.

+

In the morning, he——

stooped and stretches——
sings a song of praise
from long ago, while

a little sun strikes
a little frost
on the skin of the earth:

Some say the gate out is the river
some say the gate out is rain——
but I agree with those who say
that every gate is a gate of praise…

then the sagebrush rattles,
then out limps a tattered
sheepdog, thin and just like

that.

+
He had a father
and a mother!
His dreams were

cathedral homes
for beetles, of which
there are 450,000

different species so far
identified. Or, *Could you*
take down the heaviest

book from the top
shelf please? Read
to me more about

A is for Aviary?

he would inquire.

Now sleep is all
the cathedral he desires

please.

+

He lives on the steps
of the cathedral now.
Cardboard, wind-tug

and rattle. And sometimes
the trash does a dull
little dance. Rash,

stiff and throb
inhabit. He is
insect, rat and rust

hampered. Danger
is his host—
and all forgetting

or maybe dreaming—
or maybe just all

dreaming.

+
His hands

are bitten and grease—
one thumb
no longer performing.

At the way top
of the cathedral
the Angel Gabriel looks

out over the city
and blows his little horn—
say some, though he

thinks it could just
as well be a Native
American with a peace pipe,

*Who could possibly know
from here,* he argues.

And it is a strong
argument.

+

In the little park
behind the cathedral
he gives the stray cats

water in an old
anchovy tin when
the heat shoots up

and everybody who can
leaves town, including
the cat-volunteers.

Good thing he is there
to rinse out the tin
in the drinking fountain

and fill it again.
The cats do not
let him touch them

and when he hums
they pretend not
to listen. Sometimes

the cats eat beetles
sometimes ants, though
for eating they prefer

the warm-blooded creatures.
Either way they have
made up their minds

about certain things:
like people,
no exceptions.

+

He says he has seen
the sky and the steps
of the cathedral

and the little apple
branches that reach
over the wall

enough. He says
the thoughts
in his mind have

been in his mind
a long time now.
He doesn't have

a star, he doesn't
have a certificate
for a star. Maybe just

his mind now.

Plus a green wool hat.

Plus a crumble of cheese

for the mad dog who runs
through his memory

blinded.

+

Sometimes a deep
humming warms him
as if his heart

were a tuning fork
the world set going—.
It is not God.

It is not whiskey.
It is not even
the mad dog snoring.

It is just everything
humming the same note
at the same time—

and he is invited,

thank you.

+
Well, he whose
singing was a matter
of grave opinion

is now otherwise
employed. He is harness
and wind now, wind

and harness.

+

Sometimes a child
wanders through
the cathedral park—

looking for a lost
mitten or hat, her sitter
trailing. The stray cats

retreat and crouch
under the tangled
bushes, but they never

stop watching.

NOTES AND ACKNOWLEDGEMENTS

NOTES

HOUSE OF POURED-OUT WATERS

"Rather" is for Randall Potts.

"Talking to You" is for Julie Checkoway Thomsen.

"Notes Toward a Definition" includes quotes from or references to the following individuals and texts: Baudelaire, the Book of Job, Stonewall Jackson, John Keats, and Paul Simon.

"The Ring around the Reappearing Body": The story about Patrick is recounted in Necessary Losses by Judith Viorst. The words attributed to this true child are a direct quote. *GVW, in memoriam.*

"House of Poured-Out Waters": "House of olives," "house of mercy," and "house of poured-out waters" are different translations of Bethez, Bethesda, or Bethzatha—the pool in Jerusalem where Jesus is said to have healed a man who had been sick for thirty-eight years. "Nimitz" refers to the Nimitz Freeway, which collapsed in San Francisco's October 1989 earthquake, killing forty-two motorists. "Lisa" and "Hedda" are references to the 1988 New York City case in which Joel Steinberg was convicted of first-degree manslaughter in the beating death of his illegally adopted "daughter" Lisa, who was six at the time. Hedda Nussbaum was his partner, who had also been beaten by Steinberg. Lisa was buried in New York; her gravestone reads "GOD'S ANGEL." The italicized phrases on p. 206 are quotes from the Book of Job.

"The Prairie as Valid Provider": In the fifth section, "*By Grand Central Station I Sat Down and Wept*" is a reference to the book by that title, by Elizabeth Smart, from which the preceding two lines are a direct quote.

THE USABLE FIELD

"Gift Horizon": *Turn the head of the bird*: Just before his death, Renoir is said to have uttered these words. The poem is not specifically about Renoir.

"The High Hither, The Embrace": The title of this poem is taken from a phrase in a poem by Paul Celan.

"That Which Came of Nothing/Coming Always" is for Tina Bourjaily.

"The Crypt of the House" is for Carter Smith

"The Woman Whose Specialty Is Light—" is for my mother.

"Liminal" and "The Flesh is Fear" are for Graham de Freitas.

MONEY MONEY MONEY | WATER WATER WATER

MAGNA CARTA: The poem is composed entirely of phrases from Magna Carta.

TAMOXIFEN: Tamoxifen is a drug used to treat cancer. While taking it, my mother spoke of feeling emotionally "wooden."

Was too a story passing through: "The bird outside my sister rapture" is a variation on a line by Amanda Lichtenberg.

DUST AND RUMBLE: The Loma Prieta earthquake of 1989 was caused by slippage along the San Andreas Fault and was responsible for 69 deaths and much damage in the San Francisco Bay area.

THE MULE DEER, **: "John" refers to John Berger in *Hold Everything Dear: Dispatches on Survival and Resistance*.

"When the birds fall out of the sky / And the fish wash up on the shore" is a reference to the literal, mystifying instances of just such occurrences in recent years.

MOWING AND AFTERMATH: When mowed and disked under, mustard plant, the traditional cover crop in vineyards, produces mustard gas, which kills nematodes and other parasitic organisms.

WORLD OF MADE AND UNMADE

Artwork and Photographs:
"account books" Nancy Morgan Whitaker (p. 452)
"fish one" Nancy Morgan Whitaker (p. 481)
"fish two" Nancy Morgan Whitaker (p. 481)
Nancy Morgan Whitaker and Douglas Hunt Whitaker on bike, circa 1934, Woods Hole, MA (p. 508)

NEW POEMS

"The World Per Se": "the book on factory farming" is *Eating Animals* by Jonathan Safran Foer.

"John's Dog King/and His Little Band/of Embattled Homeless" and "He" are inspired by John Berger's novel *King*. "He" is for John Berger.

ACKNOWLEDGEMENTS

My warm thanks to the editors, publishers, and staff of the journals and anthologies in which the poems in this collection first appeared, sometimes in different versions.

THE LORD AND THE GENERAL DIN OF THE WORLD

American Poetry Review: "Delphi, Coming around the Corner," "LaGuardia, the Story," and "Passing a Truck Full of Chickens at Night on Highway Eighty"

The Antioch Review: "In Need of a World"

Arete: Forum for Thought: "On the Lawn at the Drug Rehab Center" and "To Nobody: February 20, 1985"

The Beloit Poetry Journal: "In the Parking Lot at the Junior College on the Eve of a Presidential Election"

The Boston Review: "Fall" and "Sparrow, My Sparrow"

The Iowa Review: "For Alex at the Gladman Memorial Hospital" and "To the Body"

The North Dakota Quarterly: "To Vincent Van Gogh of the House He Painted in 1890, the Year of His Death"

Pequod: "A Note on the Present State of the Future," "Begin Where We All Know Which and Where We Are," and "After Detox" (formerly "Maybe She Go")

Ploughshares: "The Case of the Misplaced Caption," "Bach, Winter," "Paradise Consists of Forty-Nine Rotating Spheres," and "Where the Zinfandel Pass Their Seasons in Mute Rows"

The Seattle Review: "Mapping the Mind"

The Virginia Quarterly Review: "Concerning That Prayer I Cannot Make," "My Father's Flesh," "The Lord and the General Din of the World," "The Man in the Poetry Lounge," and "The Memory"

"Bach, Winter" was reprinted in *1986-87: Anthology of Magazine Verse and Yearbook of American Poetry*.

"Concerning That Prayer I Cannot Make" was reprinted in *The Best American Poetry of 1990*.

"Sparrow, My Sparrow" was reprinted in *Pacific International*.

"Between Self and Century," "In Need of a World" and "The Argument against Us" appeared in *Voices on the Landscape: Contemporary Iowa Poets*.

HOUSE OF POURED-OUT WATERS

"The Future," "The Animal Messenger," "To Break the Spell Is to Invite Chaos into the Universe,"
"But What If, as Is," "Lack, the Willow," and "Lack, the Hummingbird" appeared in *American Poetry
Review.*

Ten sections from "Several Scenes in Search of the Same Explosion" appeared in *Bellingham Review.*

"Problem Performed by Shadows" appeared in *Beloit Poetry Journal.*

"The Prairie as Valid Provider" appeared on-line in *Caffeine Destiny.*

"Talking to You" appeared in *Colorado Review.*

"Notes toward a Definition" appeared in *Indiana Review.*

"However," and "What Happens" appeared in *Iowa Review.*

"The Seventh Revelation of my Thirty-Seventh Year" appeared in *Luna.*

"I Have Been Living" appeared in *The New York Times.*

"Point of Departure," "The Ring around the Reappearing Body," and "House of Poured-Out
Waters" appeared in *Pequod.*

"And All These Things Are So" appeared in *Ploughshares.*

"Rather" appeared in *Poetry Flash.*

"Wind" appeared in *Shenandoah.*

"Rather a Pale Occasion for Flowers" and "Incomplete Scenario Involving What the Voice Said"
appeared in *Sonora Review.* "Incomplete Scenario Involving What the Voice Said" also appeared
in *Bread Loaf Anthology of New American Poets.*

"The World" appeared in *TriQuarterly.*

THE USABLE FIELD

Poems first appeared, sometimes in earlier versions, in: *American Poetry Review, Blink, Canary River
Review, The Bread Loaf Anthology of New American Poets, Chicago Review, The Dirty Napkin, Electronic
Poetry Review, Excerpt, "For New Orleans" & Other Poems, Great River Review, Greensboro Review, The
Indiana Review, Joyful Noise: An Anthology of American Spiritual Poetry, Ploughshares, Poetry, Poetry Daily,
Pool, TriQuarterly, Underwood Broadside Series, Washington Square,* and *Web Del Sol.*

MONEY MONEY MONEY | WATER WATER WATER

Poems first appeared, sometimes in earlier versions, in *American Poetry Review, Columbia Poetry Review, Fifth Wednesday Journal, Great River Review, SEIZURE STATE (Gigantic), The Iowa Review, Passages North, Poetry, Poetry Daily, Poetry International, Scythe* and *Tidepools*.

WORLD OF MADE AND UNMADE

Heartfelt thanks to Rick Barot and Carolyn Kuebler for their substantial commitment to this poem, the following sections of which appeared in *New England Review:* The third time my mother fell; Outside the window the trees; In the hills above Rincon; And when there was nothing left; We are lying in the big bed; In animal darkness, before; I bring breakfast, balancing the tray; Turns out Leo is one lying; This year I have disappeared; The hornets swarm in the diesel-filled air.; *How will you spend your courage,;* From my mother's cabin I hear them —; Mexico is a snake eating; *When this is all over;* My mother's curled up on the big bed—; In my dream my mother comes with me.; Is that MY black dog—; Just after seven we turned her; the life falls shut,; The day after my mother died; And the bit about the answer.

NEW POEMS

American Poetry Review: "He"
Poetry Magazine: "The Outstretched Earth"
The Los Angeles Review of Books: "The World Per Se"
"He" was reprinted in *The Pushcart Prize Anthology 2019*

I am grateful to the Mrs. Giles Whiting Foundation, the Patrick Lannan Foundation, the John Simon Guggenheim Foundation, the Elizabeth Bishop House, and the MacDowell Colony for invaluable fellowships, grants, and residencies that have supported my writing over the years.

To everybody at Alice James Books, my great thanks for your dedication and hard work. And enduring gratitude to the friends and family whose support and love has carried me through the years: Parry, Bill, Peter, Whit, Gale, Betsey, Madeleine, Kathleen, Annie, Anne Marie, Andrea, Tess, Julie, Jerry, Jean, Lisa, Jan, Mary Ann, Rose, Silvia, Ramon, Carol, Forrest, Jane, Valyntina, Ira, The Horsewomen.

INDEX OF TITLES

INDEX OF FIRST LINES

576

About the Author

TO THE WREN collects a generous selection of new poems as well as five poetry books and a chapbook, books which have themselves been finalists for the Griffin Prize for Excellence in Poetry and The L. A. Times Book Award, and long listed for the National Book Award. Mead is the recipient of a Whiting Writer's Award, a Guggenheim Foundation Fellowship, and a Completion Grant from the Lannan Foundation. She has taught at numerous universities, including Colby College, Wake Forest University, Washington University in Saint Louis, and The Iowa Writers' Workshop. She lives and works in northern California.

© Mary S. Shea

Book Benefactors

Alice James Books wishes to thank the following individuals who generously contributed toward the publication of *To the Wren: Collected & New Poems*:

Laurie Sewall

For more information about AJB's book benefactor program, contact us via phone or email, or visit alicejamesbooks.org to see a list of forthcoming titles.

Recent Titles from Alice James Books

Angel Bones, Ilyse Kusnetz

Monsters I Have Been, Kenji C. Liu

Soft Science, Franny Choi

Bicycle in a Ransacked City: An Elegy, Andrés Cerpa

Anaphora, Kevin Goodan

Ghost, like a Place, Iain Haley Pollock

Isako Isako, Mia Ayumi Malhotra

Of Marriage, Nicole Cooley

The English Boat, Donald Revell

We, the Almighty Fires, Anna Rose Welch

DiVida, Monica A. Hand

pray me stay eager, Ellen Doré Watson

Some Say the Lark, Jennifer Chang

Calling a Wolf a Wolf, Kaveh Akbar

We're On: A June Jordan Reader, Edited by Christoph Keller and Jan Heller Levi

Daylily Called It a Dangerous Moment, Alessandra Lynch

Surgical Wing, Kristin Robertson

The Blessing of Dark Water, Elizabeth Lyons

Reaper, Jill McDonough

Madwoman, Shara McCallum

Contradictions in the Design, Matthew Olzmann

House of Water, Matthew Nienow

World of Made and Unmade, Jane Mead

Driving without a License, Janine Joseph

The Big Book of Exit Strategies, Jamaal May

play dead, francine j. harris

Thief in the Interior, Phillip B. Williams

Second Empire, Richie Hofmann

Drought-Adapted Vine, Donald Revell

Refuge/es, Michael Broek

O'Nights, Cecily Parks

Alice James Books has been publishing poetry since 1973. The press was founded in Boston, Massachusetts as a cooperative wherein authors performed the day-to-day undertakings of the press. This collaborative element remains viable even today, as authors who publish with the press are also invited to become members of the editorial board and participate in editorial decisions at the press. The editorial board selects manuscripts for publication via the press's annual, national competition, the Alice James Award. AJB remains committed to its founders' original mission to support women poets, while expanding upon the scope to include poets of all genders, backgrounds, and stages of their careers. In keeping with our efforts to foster equity and inclusivity in publishing and the literary arts, AJB seeks out poets whose writing possesses the range, depth, and ability to cultivate empathy in our world and to dynamically push against silence. The press was named for Alice James, sister to William and Henry, whose extraordinary gift for writing went unrecognized during her lifetime.

DESIGNED BY

PAMELA A. CONSOLAZIO

Spark
design

PRINTED BY MCNAUGHTON & GUNN